EXERCISE BOOK

to accompany

Rosa/Eschholz

THE WRITER'S BRIEF HANDBOOK
Sixth Edition

Kimme Nuckles
Baker College of Auburn Hills
and
Sandra Valensky
Baker College System

PEARSON
Longman

New York Boston San Francisco
London Toronto Sydney Tokyo Singapore Madrid
Mexico City Munich Paris Cape Town Hong Kong Montreal

Exercise Book to accompany Rosa/Eschholz, *The Writer's Brief Handbook, Sixth Edition*

Copyright ©2008 Pearson Education, Inc.

ISBN: 0-205-52168-1

3 4 5 6 7 8 9 10–EB–10 09 08

CONTENTS

A NOTE TO INSTRUCTORS

Thank you for adopting *The Writer's Brief Handbook* and its companion, *Exercise Book* for *The Writer's Brief Handbook*. This exercise book has been designed to help your students practice the many points made in *The Writer's Brief Handbook*. In general, for each rule in the *Handbook*, one or more exercises are presented. Most exercises contain ten problems, and answers for the first five problems are included at the back of this book. A full set of answers is available in a separate publication, entitled the *Answer Key*. Thus, your students can work independently on numbers 1—5, and the remaining problems can be used for homework, quizzes, or as additional practice for students needing help in learning a particular rule or concept.

Format

Each exercise set is explicitly keyed to the rules presented in the *Handbook*; for example, "PARTS AND PATTERNS 1a" refers you to the section "Sentence Parts and Patterns," rule 1a. In order to further help you locate material, a table of contents is also provided.

Instructors who have assigned *The Writer's Brief Handbook* as a textbook may duplicate any or all of these exercises and the answers in the *Answer Key* for distribution to students. The *Exercise Book* may also be purchased by students. In addition, the *Handbook* and the *Exercise Book* are available for purchase as a shrink-wrapped package at a special discount. Instructors interested in additional information on this package discount should call their Allyn & Bacon/Longman representative or toll-free 800-852-8024.

Also available is *The Writer's Handbook Companion Website*, located at www.ABLongman.com/Rosa. This site enables instructors to post and make changes to their syllabi; receive the scores of objective tests on grammar, punctuation and mechanics; hold chat sessions with individual students or groups of students; and receive e-mail and essay assignments directly from students.

I THE WRITING PROCESS

Using one of the following suggested topics or an instructor assigned topic, practice using two of the techniques for generating ideas and collecting information: brainstorming, asking questions, clustering, journaling, freewriting, or researching.

Topics:

- technology use in college

- returning to college as a nontraditional student

- the importance of a college education

- the influence of TV on children

- time management

- the importance of leadership skills in the workplace

Follow the model in the Handbook in sections 1d–f and 2c of chapter I.

Reflect on which technique worked best for you and that you may use in your writing process.

Now choose one of the topics for which you generated ideas and develop several thesis statements for it. Refer to chapter I, section 1f. Review the Thesis Essentials on p. 11.

Once you have developed a thesis statement for your topic, write an introduction, using one of the strategies found in section 2c of chapter I.

Imagine you have completed your essay on the selected topic. Now write a possible concluding paragraph, using one or more of the strategies in section 2c of chapter I.

WRIT PROC

4c, Proofreading   **Refer to the Handbook, pp. 26–27.**

Proofread the writing excerpt that begins on the following page. Mark up the sample essay as you would your own work, making changes on the page. There are twenty-four errors that need to be corrected.

For example:

When I travel I always, or at least usually, carry along with me at least teh following items; shaving kit, extra socks, and an extra Fifty Dollars folded inside my shoe. These items has bailed me out of more tight situations then I care to mension.

Answer:

indent 5 spaces   wdy

When I travel I always, ~~or at least usually,~~ carry along with me at

    the

: least ~~teh~~ following items; shaving kit, extra socks, and an extra Fifty

  d

Dollars folded inside my shoe. These items ~~has~~ have bailed me out of more

tight situations then I care to mension.

"The Perils Of Astroturf"

Andy Pellet

As a purist and a sports fan, I am suspicious of changes in my favorite pasttimes, namely, baseball and football. In the past too decades, there has been many new developments. Some good and some bad. But the most disturbing change is the introduction of artificial turf as a playing surface; because it makes the game's unnatural and causes injuries.

This fake grass first appeared on the sporting scene in 1966, according to the Houston Chronicle. The grass in the Houston Astrodome was dying, so in desparation it replaced by artificial turf. This new surface, manufactured by the Monsanto Company, was appropriately called "AstroTurf". Since the time of its first appearance on the sporting scene in 1966, the living grass in the stadiums and playing fields have been replaced with one form of artificial turf or another, usually made of green nylon fibers stiched over a cushioned polyester mat, AstroTurf is still the most common form.

What's so great about artificial turf? If real grass was good enough for the sports heros of yesteryear, why shouldn't it be good enough for today's? The proponents of artificial turf have two basic arguments.

The first arguement used a familiar line of reasoning: artificial turf saved money. The field needs less... .

3

ARGUE

4, Distinguishing between Fact and Opinion   **Refer to the Handbook, pp. 54–62.**

Directions: Identify which of the following statements are fact and which are opinion. (F *or* O)

1. _____ The World Trade Center tragedy affected the United States more than other countries.

2. _____ The terrorist attack on the World Trade Center could have been prevented.

3. _____ Country music is the best style of music for dancing.

4. _____ Studying history is not relevant to today's workplace.

5. _____ The legal drinking age in most states is twenty-one.

6. _____ Spending money to explore Mars is useless.

7. _____ O.J. Simpson was found not guilty of murder in 1995.

8. _____ Presidential elections should not be based on the Electoral College.

9. _____ Attending college increases a person's earning potential for a lifetime.

10. _____ The space shuttle *Challenger* exploded before landing.

ARGUE

4a, Facts versus Claims   Refer to the Handbook, pp. 54–56.

Identify each of the following statements as either a fact or a claim. If the statement is a fact, rewrite it to make the statement into a claim. If the statement is already a claim, simply label it as such.

Example:

(   ) The FCC scheduled HDTV broadcasting to begin in all major metropolitan areas of the U.S. by 2002.

In the example above, first identify the statement as a fact. Then, rewrite the sentence and convert it into a claim. One possible answer might look like this:

(fact   ) The FCC scheduled HDTV broadcasting to begin in all major metropolitan areas of the U.S. by 2002.

(claim   ) After 2002, HDTV revolutionized television broadcasting in all major metropolitan areas of the U.S.

1. (   ) Euthanasia is a right that every American should have the option of electing.

   (   )

2. (   )   Some animal rights advocates object to the use of animals for medical research and testing.

   (   )

3. (   ) The use of grades is traditional in American schools.

   (   )

4. (   ) Snowboarding became an Olympic medal sport in 1998.

   (   )

5. (   ) U.S. immigration policy changed after September 11, 2001.

   (   )

6. (   ) *Titanic* was the most expensive movie ever made.

   (   )

7. (   ) Global warming has created the conditions responsible for El Niño.

   (   )

8. (   ) U.S. Department of Transportation studies have revealed that in collisions between cars and trucks/sport utility vehicles, 80% of the fatalities occur in the cars.

   (   )

9. (   ) World hunger is a problem that will never be solved.

   (   )

10. (   ) Though 30% of all cancers are associated with tobacco use, the government has not made it an illegal substance.

   (   )

ARGUE

4b, Logical Appeals   **Refer to the Handbook, pp. 56–59.**

For each of the following sentences, identify the corresponding logical fallacy.

Example: Either you are part of the problem or part of the solution.

Answer: Either/Or Thinking

1. Every time I go to the hockey game, I come down with a cold; therefore, hockey games cause colds.

2. If everyone would be a vegetarian, no one would have health problems.

3. College is hard because there is a lot of hard work.

4. The governments of Russia and China are similar because they are near each other.

5. Everyone should try the South Beach Diet because that is what all the supermodels use.

6. No one should vote for Jean Baldwin because she smokes.

7. If the president can afford to send troops around the world, we ought to be able to find a solution to homelessness.

8. You don't care about social security ending because you're only twenty years old.

9. If you can't get an A in a class, there's no sense continuing with school.

10. Exercising will improve a person's energy because she is working out.

ONLINE WRITING

5a, E-mail   **Refer to the Handbook, pp. 66–68.**

A sample e-mail from a student to a professor appears below. The message contains twelve violations of the guidelines in chapter II- Section 5a.6 Name each of the errors in the spaces provided.

```
TO: arosa@lynx.uvm.edu

FROM: psmith@cat.uvm.edu

DATE/TIME: 24FEB02; 21:17:12

SUBJ:

Dear Prof. Rosa,

I just returned from a trip and wanted to check
w/u  on our current assignment b/c I lost my
syllabus. ; ) IS IT TRUE THAT OUR FIRST DRAFT
IS DUE MONDAY? That's wut John P told me. But
this is not enough tmie to get the paper off to a
good start. So, please let me know what's up ASAP.

TTFN,

Peter S.
```

1. _____

2. _____

3. _____

4. _____

5. _____

6. _____

7. _____

8. _____

9. _____

10. _____

11. _____

12. _____

PUBLIC WRITING

7a, Formatting a Business Letter   Refer to the Handbook, pp. 73–77.

In the following sample business letter by a student seeking employment, correct the formatting errors for each of the numbered locations. The first one is done for you as an example.

In addition, there are twelve formatting flaws in this sample page; list them and describe what should have been done instead. Use the spaces provided.

   (a) <u>top of page</u> to <u>top of return address</u>: 6–12 line spaces (use this variation to balance the letter visually on the page from top to bottom)

1. **(b)** line spacing:

2. **(c)** left margin:

3. **(d)** bottom margin:

4. **(e)** right margin:

5. appropriate letter type (full block; modified block; indented)?

6. _____

7. _____

8. _____

9. _____

10. _____

11. _____

12. _____

(1)

207 Coolidge Hall

University of Vermont

Burlington, Vermont **(5)** 05401

(2)

February 1, 2007

Mr. Harold Von Braun

(6) Director, **(7)** Management Training Center

Acme Pyrotechnics, Inc.

Tuscon, AZ 87654

Dear Mr. Von Braun, **(8)**

(3) Lorem ipsum dolor sit amet, consectetuer adipiscing elit, sed diam nonummy. Nibh euismod tincidunt ut laoreet dolore magna aliquam erat volutpat. Duis autem vel eum iriure dolor in hendrerit in vulputate velit esse molestie consequat, abitando quest'anno in toscana. Vel illum dolore eu feugiat nulla facilisis at vero eros et accumsan et iusto odio dignissim qui blandit.

(4) Ut wisi enim ad minim veniam, quis nostrud exerci tation ullamcorper suscipit lobortis nisl ut aliguip ex ea commodo consequat. Duis autem vel eum iriure dolor in hendrerit in vulputate. Velit esse molestie consequat, vel illum dolore eu feugiat nulla facilisis at vero eros et accumsan et iusto odio dignissim qui blandit praesent luptatum.

Ut wisi enim ad minim veniam.

Sincerely Yours **(9) (10) (11)**

William C. Aiote

Enclosure Resume **(12)**

III PARAGRAPHS

PARA
1, Unity

Refer to the Handbook, pp. 83–87.

Examine each of the following sample paragraphs for unity. First underline the topic sentence of each paragraph. Then cross out any words, phrases, or clauses in the paragraph that do not develop the topic sentence.

For example:

The most important day I remember in all my life is the one on which my teacher, Anne Mansfield Sullivan, came to me. I am filled with wonder when I consider the immeasurable contrast between the two lives that it connects. It was the third of March, 1887, three months before I was seven years old. The spring had been seasonable and pleasant.

Answer:

<u>The most important day I remember in all my life is the one on which my teacher, Anne Mansfield Sullivan, came to me.</u> I am filled with wonder when I consider the immeasurable contrast between the two lives that it connects. It was the third of March, 1887, three months before I was seven years old. ~~The spring had been seasonable and pleasant.~~

—modified from Helen Keller, *The Story of My Life*

1. Mental models, our conceptual models of the ways objects work, events take place, or people behave, result from our tendency to form explanations of things. These models are essential in helping us understand our experiences, predict the outcomes of our actions, and handle unexpected occurrences. Unexpected occurrences can happen at any time. We base our models on whatever knowledge we have, real or imaginary, naïve or sophisticated.

—modified from Donald Norman, *The Psychology of Everyday Things*

12

2. The market is as much a part of your company as you are. After all, it represents one-half of the ledger. To grow, your business must earn the permission of the marketplace. No concept is more important for the start-up entrepreneur. Guarantees are an essential component. Customers must give your business permission to sell to them. They do this (at least as repeat customers) only after a thorough assessment of you, your product or service, and your operation. This is why Detroit is having trouble selling cars even though they're better built than they were. Fortunately this hasn't been a problem in the U.S. aerospace industry. These cars have to overcome years of bad notices. It will take time to accomplish this. In fact, it may take until there's a complete turnover in the market—until those of us who now think Japanese or German no longer drive.

   —modified from Paul Hawken, *Growing a Business*

3. A classical understanding sees the world primarily as underlying form itself. A romantic understanding sees it primarily in terms of immediate appearance. If you were to show an engine or a mechanical drawing or an electronic schematic to a romantic it is unlikely he would see much in it. It has no appeal because the reality he sees is its surface. Dull, complex lists of names, lines and numbers. Nothing interesting. Classification systems may say more about their creators than about the objects being classified. But if you were to show the same blueprint or schematic or give the same description to a classical person, he might look at it and then become fascinated by it because he sees that within the lines and shapes and symbols is a tremendous richness of underlying form.

   —modified from Robert Pirsig, *Zen and the Art of Motorcycle Maintenance*

4. At a certain season of our life we are accustomed to consider every spot as the possible site of a house. I have thus surveyed the country on every side within a dozen miles of where I live. In imagination I have bought all the farms in succession, for all were to be bought, and I knew their price. I enjoy walking and find it a healthful relaxation. I walked over each farmer's premises, tasted his wild apples, discoursed on husbandry with him, and took his farm at his price.

   —modified from Henry David Thoreau, *Walden*

5. As the rules of chess define the game of chess, linguistic rules define the game of language, which would not exist without them. They are not strict mechanisms of cause and effect—one thing simply making another thing happen—but a system essentially open and incomplete, so that it is always capable of novelty. Rules of etiquette close off a system, keeping it uniform and predictable unless the rules are changed. Who is allowed to change these rules? When can such changes be made? Rules of language are indirect and can be used again and again on the same finite set of letters and words, making possible an open universe of new sentences on the closed universe of the dictionary. Dictionaries, you will have noticed, are printed, not spoken.

   —modified from Jeremy Campbell, *Grammatical Man*

6. Macintosh Way marketing is the *marketing of technology*— finding the right people and getting the right information into their hands. The cost of this approach is not important. Frequently businesses take other strategies which yield different results. The foundation of this approach is that customers have a deep understanding of what they want, how things should work, and what they are willing to tolerate. They are attracted, not intimidated, by innovation and technology. They actually use and like great products.

    —modified from Guy Kawasaki, *The Macintosh Way*

7. The relative strengths of the leading nations in world affairs never remain constant, principally because of the uneven rate of growth among different societies and of the technological and organizational breakthroughs which bring a greater advantage to one society than to another. If, however, too large a proportion of the state's wealth is diverted from wealth creation and allocated instead to military purposes, then that is likely to lead to a weakening of national power over the longer term. Population growth has not shown a demonstrable effect in this pattern of controlled growth.

    —modified from Paul Kennedy, *The Rise and Fall of the Great Powers*

8. The stock market crash of 1929 brought to light substantial inadequacies in financial reporting. Investigations of bankrupt companies showed numerous arithmetic errors and cases of undetected fraud. The status of healthy companies is largely unknown. The investigations also disclosed the common use of a widely varying set of accounting practices. The 1920s were arguably a time of greater freedom. A principal outcome of these investigations was that the newly formed Securities and Exchange Commission (SEC) required that publicly held companies must annually issue a report to shareholders. The reports are generally distributed via Second or Third Class delivery. The report must contain financial statements prepared by the firm's management and audited by a certified public accountant (CPA).

    —modified from Steven Winkler, *The Complete Guide to Finance & Accounting for Nonfinance Managers*

9. Scarcely twenty miles divide Zanzibar from the African mainland, and on a clear day you can plainly see the island from the coast. A motor launch accomplishes the journey across the straits in an hour or two and makes a sound frequently reported as terrifying by the local inhabitants. By air the trip is a matter of ten or fifteen minutes. Yet there is an astonishing difference between the island and the mainland shore. In Zanzibar everything is soft and beguiling. The currents in this region are swift. Zanzibar is as relaxing as a Turkish bath.

    —modified from Alan Moorehead, *The White Nile*

10. Throughout the inhabited world, in all times and under every circumstance, the myths of man have flourished; and they have been the living inspiration of whatever else may have appeared out of the activities of the human body and mind. It is not appropriate to consider our physical beings as mere biology. It would not be too much to say that myth is the secret opening through which inexhaustible energies of the cosmos pour into human cultural manifestation. Business is not included in this analysis. Religions, philosophies, arts, the social forms of primitive and historic man, prime discoveries in science and technology, the very dreams that blister sleep, boil up from the basic, magic ring of myth. Anthropologists sometimes are the ones to carry out this investigative work.

—modified from Joseph Campbell, *The Hero with a Thousand Faces*

PARA

2b, Development Strategies 1   Refer to the Handbook, pp. 88–94.

There are many methods of developing and organizing information both within paragraphs and the essay as a whole. For example:

Narration: telling a story, most often relating events in chronological order.

Description: describing scenes, most often ordering the items spatially, as a movie camera might capture a scene.

Examples and illustration: citing examples.

Facts, statistics, reasons: using factual information, including numerical summaries.

Definition: providing an extended definition.

Process analysis: explaining a procedure, usually in a step-by-step description.

Comparison and contrast: comparing two things (demonstrating their similarities) and/or contrasting things (demonstrating their dissimilarities).

Analogy: comparing a complex or unfamiliar subject to another topic typically more widely known and understood.

Classification: grouping topics into larger classes on the basis of one or more criteria that demonstrate shared similarities.

Cause and effect: explaining the causal link between two or more subjects.

Mixed strategies: employing more than one of the preceding strategies. Many of the paragraphs in the preceding exercise use mixed strategies.

Referring to the sample paragraphs on pages 12–15, list the development strategy(ies) you think the author uses.

For example: Helen Keller, *The Story of My Life*

Answer: narration _____

1. Donald Norman, *The Psychology of Everyday Things:*

   _____

2. Paul Hawken, *Growing a Business:*

   _____

3. Robert Pirsig, *Zen and the Art of Motorcycle Maintenance:*

   _____

4. Henry David Thoreau, *Walden:*

   _____

5. Jeremy Campbell, *Grammatical Man:*

   _____

6. Guy Kawasaki, *The Macintosh Way:*

   _____

7. Paul Kennedy, *The Rise and Fall of the Great Powers:*

   _____

8. Steven Winkler, *The Complete Guide to Finance & Accounting for Nonfinance Managers:*

_____

9. Alan Moorehead, *The White Nile:*

_____

10. Joseph Campbell, *The Hero with a Thousand Faces:*

_____

PARA

2b, Development Strategies 2   Refer to the Handbook, pp. 88–94.

For each writing assignment listed here, provide one or more development strategies that you could successfully employ to write on that topic. (If necessary, refer to the list of development strategies on pages 15–16.)

For example: Explain the concept of separation of power within the U.S. government.

Answer: definition; illustration

1. Explain how NCAA basketball has changed in the last decade.

2. Discuss the operations of United Nations' peacekeeping forces.

3. Explain the slower-than-expected adoption of recycling.

4. Describe the impact on the U.S. economy of both the budget surplus and the national debt.

5. Describe the most important day in your life.

6. Describe the differences between attending college as an 18-year-old compared to returning to school as an adult.

7. Explain what a family is.

8. What is privacy in the electronic age?

9. Discuss homelessness in America.

10. Discuss changes in automobile manufacturing.

PARA

3, Coherence

Refer to the Handbook, pp. 94–99.

Writers use four principal tools to make their writing coherent: organization, transitions, repetition of key words and phrases, and parallel structures.

After reading the following passage complete the exercises that follow it.

When I was fourteen, my father's last reassignment took my whole family to Kenya for nearly two years. We arrived right after New Year's Day. Our new home, "the station," was twenty-eight miles out into the bush, and every other Saturday my parents, my sister, and I made the long drive into town. The road was rough, a rutted trail in some places, and our Land Rover ground along at never more than thirty miles an hour, all of us sweltering in this mechanical beast. It was an adventure the first few trips, but became a misery after that. On the Saturday just before our first Easter, we were again making the drive, everyone slapping about inside like raggedy dolls, and no one speaking because it was too noisy and because our moods were too close to foul. Suddenly my father yelled "Look," and pointed off to the left side.

He threw in the clutch and we coasted. Everyone in the truck turned to watch. A herd of bok had appeared on the hillside along the road and they were running full tilt. Before I could even finish asking myself why, the reason appeared: a cheetah, running at top speed. Furiously fast but so smooth it seemed to be riding on an invisible rail, the cat cut across the hill, arcing for a trailing bok. And even as I leaned forward to see better, it was already over: down went the cheetah and bok, the cheetah with his jaws wrapped around his prey's throat. Neither animal seemed to struggle. They lay suddenly still together, in a strange embrace. I could hear nothing but the sound of our engine. The two animals did not move, their silent dance of dust and speed and sere grass was done.

"Won't see much of that round here in a few years," said my father, letting the clutch back out too quickly, lurching the Rover. My head bounced hard on the door pillar.

"Ow," I yelled. I pressed my fingers to my right temple, and almost immediately a welt began to rise against my fingertips. The lump felt hot and wet. Was it blood or sweat? Overcoming this distraction, I called out to my father, "Why? I mean, why not?"

"Poaching," said my father without emotion, driving on. I strained in my seat, looking back through the mud-splattered windows, holding my head. The two animals were now out of sight, obscured by the grass. I continued to look back for another several minutes. My family rode on without speaking, the Rover grinding steadily through the landscape.

—Christopher Bray, "Voyages from Home"

1. How is the sample passage organized? (Chronologically? Spatially? Logically?) Explain your choice.

2. Underline the transitional words and phrases in the story. How do they relate to the type of organization used by the author?

For section 4 of chapter III, regarding additional examples of beginning and ending paragraphs, refer to chapter I, The Writing Process, section 2, Writing a Draft, Part C, Writing the Beginning and Ending.

IV   SENTENCE CLARITY AND STYLE

CLARITY AND STYLE

1, Parallelism

Refer to the Handbook, pp. 101–102.

Rewrite the following sentences to improve their parallel structure.

For example: Planes and trains are usually on time, and buses are, too.

Correction: Planes, trains, and buses are all usually on time.

1. We will see Rufus on Tuesday, and then Wednesday we are going to see Tito.

2. Though he could not swim, a life jacket was something he would not wear.

3. El Niño has remained active in the Pacific, and the rain continues to fall.

4. Congress does not think enough about the individual citizen, and it forgets about personal responsibility.

5. As the sun rose, the moon was setting.

6. Our team is well prepared and has great equipment; our coach too is excellent, and we've had a lot of practices.

7. I see a great future ahead, while in the past our record has been admirable.

8. He wanted to be on the stage, but he knew neither how to act nor singing.

9. Is it better to stand fast on environmental policy than having a compromise in order to save jobs?

10. At the local Kwik-Gas she is the manager, and she is also our class valedictorian.

CLARITY AND STYLE

2, Misplaced and Dangling Modifiers   Refer to the Handbook, pp. 102–104.

Rewrite the following sentences to eliminate the misplaced and dangling modifiers.

For example: Jim could see the fish jumping from the campsite.

Correction: From the campsite, Jim could see the fish jumping.

1. Don returned the tools to Phil covered with grease.

2. Threatened with extinction, the EPA wrote new rules for the spotted owl.

3. I saw him on the walkway painted green.

4. Young and inexperienced jobs were few and far between, Jim discovered.

5. I wrote directions for my friend to the house.

6. Prized by many, Leon won the award.

7. I saw a big fish with my mask and snorkel on.

8. It was so hot that I watched Owen Wilson and Vince Vaughn dressed only in my shorts in *The Wedding Crashers*.

9. I gave Della a book in the library written by Faulkner.

10. I could see Mt. Rushmore coming over the hill.

CLARITY AND STYLE

3a, Shifts 1   **Refer to the Handbook, pp. 104–105.**

Correct the inappropriate shifts in person or number in the following sentences. Indicate the type of shift you are correcting.

For example: I have played basketball at the YMCA for years. We like their courts.

Correction: **I have played basketball at the YMCA for years. I like their courts. (number)**

1. The United Nations' membership has grown steadily, and they add one or more new members nearly every year.

2. When you study, one needs to work for at least three hours.

3. Once people swim in this lake, especially in August, you never want to swim anywhere else.

4. My father worked for forty-two years at General Motors; they made him retire last month.

5. When a person takes the train to St. Louis, they should leave by 10:37.

6. Although one prepared for the storm, I was nonetheless scared by its strength.

7. It is crucial for students to study regularly so you don't get behind.

8. Denise reminded us to be sure to come early so they could get a good seat.

9. When I asked Nelson about the Baseball Hall of Fame, he said that they are located in Cooperstown, NY.

10. I remembered his advice that one has to swing smoothly in order to hit well.

CLARITY AND STYLE

3b, Shifts 2   Refer to the Handbook, pp. 105.

Correct the inappropriate shifts in verb tense.

For example: I think she is coming with us, but she wasn't.

Correction: I thought she was coming with us, but she wasn't.

OR: I think she is coming with us, but she isn't.

1.   The Mississippi River carries soil that traveled to other bodies of water.

2.   At exactly midnight, the fireworks display started, music played, and a gunshot rings in the New Year.

3.   Tomorrow we will walk to school but rode the bus home.

4.   Dogs love to play with their tails, which they chased around in circles.

5.   While Melissa washes her hair, the doorbell rang.

6.   No one cares if the game would be lost.

7.   My teacher questioned whether the class has read the chapter.

8.   Marlena looks sadly at the mess in her room before she cleaned off her bed.

9.   The interviewer asks interesting questions as soon as the celebrity has taken her seat.

10. If the organization collected donations, it will have to distribute the money equally.

CLARITY AND STYLE

3d, Shifts 3   **Refer to the Handbook, pp. 106.**

Correct the inappropriate shifts in subject or voice. Indicate the type of shift you are correcting.

For example: We noticed the hurricane damage as the town was approached.

Correction: **We noticed the hurricane damage as we approached the town. (subject)**

1. I went to the new restaurant on Elm Street, and we enjoyed the meal.

2. The newspaper was read by the entire class, and then we discussed it.

3. Reading the newspaper, the story was interesting to me.

4. Broken down, we sat until the Transit Authority sent a replacement bus.

5. The family went to the beach to swim. Playing in the sand was fun, too.

6. When we met at the Java Joint, the film was our main topic of discussion.

7. The luck of the draw was missed by my father, but he still played the lottery.

8. Running up the stairs, the book was dropped.

9. The point of diminishing returns was approached as Congress continued to modify the bill.

10. If someone wants to learn to read faster and better, it can be done through practice.

CLARITY AND STYLE

4a, Irrelevant Detail   **Refer to the Handbook, pp. 108.**

Edit the following sentences to eliminate irrelevant detail.

For example: The author's second novel, nearly four hundred pages long, did not receive the widespread acclaim of her first.

Correction: The author's second novel did not receive the widespread acclaim of her first.

1. Marx said that religion is the opium of the people, which is, I think, a strong opinion.

2. Charles Dickens, who died in 1870, was a prolific author, working on up to three novels- at the same time.

3. In the last six months, our newly elected president, who has a cocker spaniel, has created 2.6 million jobs.

4. Last Thanksgiving Chuck, who is my best friend, visited his relatives.

5. The interstate highway system, originally constructed for reasons of national security, is now badly in need of extensive rebuilding.

6. Whenever the wind blows from the north, which is actually quite often, the windows in our apartment whistle.

7. The area between the Ohio and Mississippi rivers, home many years ago to Native Americans, once was known as the West.

8. Sponsored each year by a number of local organizations, our class trip to the U.N. was fascinating.

9. My brother, who loves to read, was just elected captain of the basketball team.

10. When I read Dan Brown's *The Da Vinci Code*, it was during finals week, and I enjoyed it.

CLARITY AND STYLE

4b, Mixed or Illogical Constructions   **Refer to the Handbook, pp. 108–110.**

Edit the following sentences to eliminate mixed or illogical constructions.

For example: The reason why the baby cried is because her diaper needed changing.

Correction: **The baby cried because her diaper needed changing.**

1. He said that the new bridge won't increase nobody's taxes.

2. They chatted like two birds until they ran out of steam.

3. The baker made a triple chocolate cake; however, they forgot to add baking powder.

4. My brother wrote me a letter last week, and I read them two or three times.

5. I don't know nothing about Wagner's opera *Parsifal*.

6. They came in waves like a herd of elephants.

7. The coach gave us six new plays that was designed to confuse their defense.

8. Martin Luther King, Jr., his speeches powerful, always captured the attention of his audiences.

9. Love is where a person can't think of anyone else.

10. The reason why abortion is such a controversial issue is because many people have different values.

CLARITY AND STYLE

5a, Subordination—Choppy Sentences   Refer to the Handbook, pp. 110–111.

Using subordination, rewrite each set of short sentences as one sentence.

For example: The day was dreary. We went fishing anyway.

Rewritten: Although the day was dreary, we went fishing anyway.

1. Bill and Metsa have dated for five years. They started in high school. They think they will get married next year.

2. Dwayne Wade is fast. He plays both offense and defense well. He can play both because of his speed.

3. Our university library has over one million volumes. It covers most areas of information in depth. It also has information that is up-to-date. I do most of my research there.

4. Heat the sauce over a low flame. Stir constantly. Be sure that the butter does not brown.

5. The Statue of Liberty once again looks beautiful. It was a gift from the French people. It was dedicated in 1886. It was restored for its centennial. It is more than one hundred years old.

6. I meet Sala for lunch every Friday. I enjoy talking with her.

7. Luke studied all weekend for the exam. He was tired. He did well on the exam on Monday.

8. The sun was hot. The humidity was high. It had been this way for two weeks. John wouldn't even play baseball.

9. My mother is a Stones' fan. My father is a Beatles' fan. They are both diehards. They still argue over which group is better. I have to listen to these childish discussions.

10. My sister is tall. She is strong. She is a team player. She was elected captain of the volleyball team.

CLARITY AND STYLE

5c, Coordination—Ideas of Equal Importance   **Refer to the Handbook, pp. 112.**

Using coordination, rewrite each set of short sentences as one sentence.

For example: The U.S. economy is very complex. The Federal Reserve Board has a difficult job.

Rewritten: The U.S. economy is very complex, so the Federal Reserve Board has a difficult job.

1. I had a lot of reading to do every day. I did not watch television at all for months.

2. She agrees with many things Roberto tells her. She argues with him when she does not.

3. My great-uncle does not smoke. He also does not drink.

4. He likes classical music. He also likes country and western.

5. This rain is good for people. It is filling the reservoirs.

6. At the heart of brewing is yeast. It converts sugars to alcohol and carbon dioxide.

7. We grow a garden every summer. We eat fresh vegetables every day.

8. I generally agree with Professor Tellman's theories. I am still unsure about some of his research.

9. I can take the 7:10 train. I can catch the 7:20 bus.

10. Einstein created a mathematical formula. Einstein changed our whole concept of math.

CLARITY AND STYLE

6b, Logical Order   **Refer to the Handbook, pp. 112.**

Rewrite each of the following sentences to improve its logical and/or climactic sequence.

For example: Franco passed the bar exam, studied hard, and was hired by a prestigious
law firm.

Rewritten: Franco studied hard, passed the bar exam, and was hired by a
prestigious law firm.

1. We arrived at the Grand Canyon, hiked to the Colorado River a mile below, and loaded our packs.

2. Bonds had a terrible day when we were at the ball park; he struck out in the first, seventh, and fifth innings.

3. I like a movie if it has a good story, ends happily, and begins well.

4. In the next three hours I need to dress for a date, shower and shave, and mow the lawn.

5. As I looked at the Statue of Liberty, I saw the torch, her feet, and the crown.

6. After landing in Houston, Marty picked up his luggage, drove into the city, and rented a car.

7. The thunderstorm raced in, the clouds turned gray, and a rainbow appeared.

8. To pay your monthly bills, first write the checks, then deposit the money in your account, and then figure which bills to pay.

9. John began his research paper by reading on his topic, taking notes, and finding a topic.

10. When I get ready for work, I pack my lunch, get out of bed, and start the car.

CLARITY AND STYLE

6c, Active Voice   **Refer to the Handbook, pp. 113.**

Rewrite the following sentences to change the active voice to the passive voice or vice versa.

For example: Fresh peas were loved by Julie. (passive voice)

Rewritten: Julie loved fresh peas. (active voice)

1. Mosquitoes, black flies, and chiggers bit Paul on his canoe trip down the Allagash River.

2. The ball was hit deep to center by Rodriguez.

3. A new puppy was bought by the family.

4. Everyone in our dorm celebrated Kurt's birthday.

5. I was called by Patrick as soon as he returned to Seattle.

6. Carol sang "The Star-Spangled Banner" at the opening game of the Detroit Red Wings.

7. Many immigrants were examined by the U.S. Naturalization Service at Ellis Island.

8. Angela was read *Goodnight Moon* by her parents as a child.

9. Now Angela reads *Goodnight Moon* to Rosauro every night.

10. Maya's report was praised by her boss.

CLARITY AND STYLE

7a, Sentence Variety 1   **Refer to the Handbook, pp. 115.**

Rewrite the following sentences to eliminate the overuse of short, simple sentences.

For example: Darif had a great day. He was early for class. He got an A on his midterm. He received a birthday card from his parents.

Rewritten: Darif was early for class, got an A on his midterm, and received a birthday card from his parents, making it a great day.

1. It rained for a month. There was great flooding.

2. Vermont has a long winter. It seems shorter now that I ski.

3. My parents sang in church every Sunday for years. Last year they stopped. They miss it now.

4. Fly over any major U.S. city. Look out the plane's window. You will be shocked by the number of swimming pools you will see.

5. Anne gets up at 5 a.m. every day. She never misses her gymnastics practice.

6. A house has many main parts. It has a foundation. It has a frame. It has a roof. It has internal systems—such as electricity and plumbing.

7. I heard Lazlo's newest album on the radio. It's another hit, I think.

8. Every morning I get up. I exercise. I shower and dress. I carpool to work.

9. Howard read an article about government waste. It made him feel frustrated.

10. A new mall was proposed. It raised many questions. One of them was whom would it benefit.

CLARITY AND STYLE

7b, Sentence Variety 2   **Refer to the Handbook, pp. 116–117.**

Rewrite sentences A and B to begin with the structure indicated.

Given: Roland and Lynda walked in the park and forgot about all their cares for the evening.

Begin with an infinitive: To forget about all their cares for the evening, Roland and Lynda walk in the park.

Begin with a participle: Forgetting about all their cares for the evening, Roland and Lynda walked in the park.

Begin with a subordinate clause: Because they wanted to forget about all their cares for the evening, Roland and Lynda walked in the park.

Begin with a prepositional phrase: In the park, Roland and Lynda walked to forget about all their cares for the evening.

A. Sally wrote her research paper and handed it in to her teacher to fulfill the course requirements in Composition I.

1. *Begin with an infinitive*:

2. *Begin with a participle*:

3. *Begin with a subordinate clause*:

4. *Begin with a prepositional phrase*:

B: Samuel de Champlain discovered a great freshwater lake, and claimed it for France to please the king in 1609.

5. *Begin with an infinitive*:

6. *Begin with a participle:*

7. *Begin with a subordinate clause:*

8. *Begin with a prepositional phrase*:

V   WORD CHOICE

WORD

1, Eliminating Clutter   Refer to the Handbook, pp. 119–121.

Rewrite each of the following wordy sentences to make them concise and direct.

Example: Good, clear instructions eliminate, I think, a lot of possible confusion later.

Rewritten: **Clear instructions eliminate later confusion.**

1. I'd say that Tom was basically a point guard that can, when he's got to, play center.

2. I thought that the test was really hard on account of the fact that we had to know in essence everything from the whole semester.

3. Due to the fact that there was bad weather in Atlanta, Bill's two brothers, who were flying, were delayed, and we had to wait at the airport for them for five hours.

4. The school band, which it seems to me obviously hadn't practiced enough, couldn't even play the national anthem without mistakes.

5. Can you explain why it is that schools of fish, which live in the water, and flocks of birds that fly in the air, move as a single group with similar coordinated motions?

6. The trees on my street, which are of three different types, all change color in fall at what I would estimate to be the very same time.

7. The governor, who was popular and who was already serving his third term in office, was given yet another vote of confidence at the polls by the voting populace at election time.

8. In spite of the fact that Orlo, who is conductor of our orchestra, was late, the concert began virtually on time.

9. While everyone's point of view, and ideas, and feelings must be taken into account and assessed carefully and thoughtfully, it seems to me that in the end the president is kind of charged with the task of leading rather than evaluating.

10. Barbara Walters, for all intents and purposes, is a great interviewer for the simple reason that she is pointed with her questions, and she will long be remembered for that.

WORD

2c, General versus Specific Words

Refer to the Handbook, pp. 124–125.

For each general word in the list, provide a specific example.

Example: emotions: **happiness**

1. transportation:

2. foods:

3. vegetables:

4. seasons:

5. holidays:

6. colors:

7. metals:

8. trees:

9. music:

10. birds:

WORD

2c, Abstract versus Concrete Words
Refer to the Handbook, pp. 124–125.

Identify each word in the following list as either abstract or concrete.

Example: emotions: **abstract**

1. pretty:

2. justice:

3. leaves:

4. blue:

5. stars:

6. wood:

7. fast:

8. cake:

9. truth:

10. shoes:

11. paper:

12. bright:

13. fun:

14. rock:

15. tall:

16. new:

17. slippery:

18. wind:

19. music:

20. juice:

WORD

2d, Idioms   **Refer to the Handbook, pp. 125–126.**

Correct the misuse of prepositions in the following sentences containing idiomatic expressions.

Example: I am concerned for your attitude.

Correction: I am concerned about your attitude.

1. The committee agreed with the plan.

2. Frieda left early so that she would be sure and get a good seat.

3. My niece insisted that Jell-O was superior than pudding.

4. Though we arrived early, we still had to wait on line.

5. The coach gave me some extra tips to help me try and improve my shot.

6. Their route was different than ours.

7. The House of Representatives was angry at the Senate's resolution.

8. Jazz is Hector's favorite type of a music.

9. When dancing with a partner, try not to vary to the beat.

10. Houston Street is parallel from Canal Street.

WORD

3a-e, Appropriate Formality   **Refer to the Handbook, pp. 128–131.**

Rewrite each of the following sentences, substituting the italicized word or phrase with a more formal expression.

Example: Gerald *took off* after work.

Answer: Gerald left after work.

1. Reggie *couldn't stand* their new album.

2. Bryan *can't* come today.

3. The show was *really cool.*

4. Collecting stamps was Phil's *thing.*

5. If I have time, *I'll catch a bite* with you at noon.

6. What *stuff* did Professor Higgins *talk about* today?

7. K.C. said, *"Don't dis your sis."*

8. When *I'm done, I'm gonna cruise to* Ridley's Café.

9. Rickie decided *to hang* in the library *til* I finished.

10. Ozzie *shot the breeze* with Harriet on the porch.

WORD

4, Bias in Writing

Refer to the Handbook, pp. 131–133.

Rewrite each of the following sentences to eliminate sexist terminology.

Example: Suzanne Porter was the anchorman on our local news.

Answer: Suzanne Porter was the anchor on our local news.

1. Our firemen showed great courage while battling the blaze.

2. The president was swamped with questions from the newsmen.

3. The safety course was tailored to mailmen.

4. Who's chairman of that Senate subcommittee?

5. Of all creatures on the planet, man is the most intelligent and the most destructive.

6. My bag is so heavy that I hope the hotel has a bellboy.

7. My sister-in-law is a policeman.

8. The job was so big that Laura was not sure our department had enough manpower to complete the work on time.

9. The plane was full, and the stewardesses had to hustle throughout the flight.

10. All the congressmen are happy to be re-elected.

WORD

5, The Dictionary   Refer to the Handbook, pp. 133–136.

Use a dictionary to answer the following questions.

1. How many syllables are in *oblivious* and *obnoxious?* Write out both words and mark the syllable breaks.

2. Define *marathon* and explain the origin of the word.

3. What is the etymology of the word *lens?* What type of lens best exemplifies this origin?

4. What is the origin of the word *frankfurter?*

5. How many syllables are in *scrupulous?* Write out the word and mark the syllable breaks.

6. Check the etymology of the word *bait.* You will find that it is a particular form of a related word that is also found in English. What is that other word?

7. What are the two meanings of the noun *chamois?* What are the variant spellings of this word?

8. What is the origin of the name of the game *hop-scotch?*

9. How has the word *apron* changed over time? (Hint: What is faulty separation?) Give a similar word that did not undergo this same change.

10. What is it that makes a *March hare* mad?

WORD

6, The Thesaurus

Refer to the Handbook, pp. 136.

For each word given, use a thesaurus to find five or more synonyms and at least one antonym. Indicate the part of speech for your entries.

Example: probe

Answer: Noun: investigation; inquiry; examination; exploration; research; scrutiny: study

Verb: explore; delve; dig; penetrate

antonym: (noun) cover-up

1. beautiful

2. show

3. nice

4. document

5. industrious

6. riot

7. hot

8. consolidate

9. said

10. assure

PARTS & PATTERNS

1a, Verbs   **Refer to the Handbook, pp. 137–138.**

For each of the sentences, underline the verb once. Then indicate if the verb expresses action or a state of being as follows:

- If the verb is linking, underline both the verb and the predicate adjective(s) or predicate noun(s) (VI, PA, PN).

- If the action verb is transitive, underline both the verb and the indirect or direct object(s) (VT, IO, DO).

- If the action verb is intransitive, underline only the verb (VI).

For example: Ollie cut the boards.
                    VT   DO

1. Tina swims in the pool on Tuesdays.

2. John gave Fred a birthday present.

3. The weather seems fine today.

4. Shelby bought her textbooks at the campus bookstore.

5. Jorge is a tenor.

6. Bread was delivered to the flood victims by the National Guard.

7. The National Guard gave the flood victims bread.

8. Biotechnology has required a very substantial investment.

9. Nanna wrote me a long letter.

10. Barbara sings for her church choir.

PARTS & PATTERNS

1a, Nouns   **Refer to the Handbook, pp. 139–140.**

Complete the following table. Consult a dictionary if necessary.

For example:

	SINGULAR	PLURAL	SINGULAR POSSESSIVE	PLURAL POSSESSIVE
	pen	**pens**	**pen's**	**pens'**
1.	dish			
2.	hero			
3.	book			
4.	wife			
5.	man			
6.	boss			
7.	fish			
8.	roof			
9.	sky			
10.	society			

PARTS & PATTERNS

1a, Pronouns   **Refer to the Handbook, pp. 140–141.**

Underline the pronouns in the following sentences.

For example: Doris gave <u>it</u> to <u>me</u>, but <u>I</u> told <u>her</u> <u>it</u> wasn't <u>mine</u>.

1. I gave Donald a call.

2. I spoke to him yesterday.

3. He usually has to call me back.

4. Raspberries are ready at their farm.

5. Which farm do you visit?

6. Each of the girls has her book.

7. I often go to the library by myself.

8. Our teacher reminded us to begin our research papers early.

9. Josie's paper on recycling was more interesting than mine.

10. Because the Guggenheim Museum was closed, we went to the Whitney.

PARTS & PATTERNS

1a, Adjectives   **Refer to the Handbook, pp. 141.**

Choose the correct adjectival form (positive, comparative, or superlative) and underline your selection in each sentence that follows.

For example: Is the Empire State Building still the world's (tall, taller, <u>tallest</u>)?

1. If presented with Häagen-Daz and Ben & Jerry's ice creams, could you say which is (creamy, creamier, creamiest)?

2. The *Washington Post* declined to name the (good, better, best) candidate among the five potential nominees.

3. Jack is (old, older, oldest) than his brother John.

4. Jack is the (old, older, oldest) of the four children.

5. Before starting the race, the judge called, "May the (good, better, best) cyclist win!"

6. I've eaten a lot of good strawberry shortcakes, but I still think my mom's is (good, better, best).

7. Khalil and Sollie can never agree which is (fun, more fun, the most fun)—Manhattan Beach or Rockaway Beach.

8. The meteorologist said that yesterday may have been hot, but today would be (hot, hotter, hottest).

9. He also said that last Thursday was the (hot, hotter, hottest) day this summer.

10. Cora told me that the Everglades were (big, bigger, biggest) than Okefenokee Swamp and Great Dismal Swamp.

PARTS & PATTERNS

1a, Adverbs **Refer to the Handbook, pp. 141–142.**

Underline the adverbs in the following sentences.

For example: Things cook <u>more</u> <u>slowly</u> in Denver than Dallas because of the altitude.

1. John runs fast.

2. Of all the sopranos, Lena sang the most beautifully.

3. The commute home always seemed longer than the one to the office.

4. After the thunderstorm, steam rose eerily from the still-warm pavement.

5. Jackson was tired but worked hard to finish the assigned reading before going to bed.

6. For a work so famous, Lincoln's "Gettysburg Address" is surprisingly short.

7. High-speed rail may change how frequently we fly to Los Angeles.

8. Ellen was very happy to discover that the most important book in her bibliography had not been checked out of the library.

9. The children of immigrants rarely know much about their parents' homeland.

10. The vase of freshly cut peonies gave the room a wonderful smell.

PARTS & PATTERNS

1a, Prepositions   **Refer to the Handbook, pp. 142.**

In the following sentences, enclose the complete prepositional phrases in parentheses and underline the prepositions.

For example: I walked (<u>to</u> the grocery, the fruit stand, and the bank).

1. On the move since dawn, the hikers had advanced twenty miles by lunchtime.

2. Sara finished three of the four essay questions quickly.

3. Chu's nieces and nephews danced around the room.

4. Bill saw his quarter roll into the street and disappear down a storm drain.

5. Forty-seven stories above the street, the birds built their nest on one of the Chrysler Building's ledges.

6. After delivering the newspapers, Susan realized her hands were black with ink.

7. The river wound its way into town from the east.

8. In the excitement, I couldn't remember who came after me in the lineup.

9. *Holes* is still one of Harlin's favorites.

10. Carol's hook shot bounced off the rim just after the buzzer sounded.

PARTS & PATTERNS

1a, Conjunctions   **Refer to the Handbook, pp. 142–143.**

In the following sentences, enclose the conjunction-containing clauses in parentheses. Then underline the conjunctions and label them as coordinating (COORD), subordinating (SUB), or correlative (CORREL).

For example: (<u>If</u> I had more money), I would replace my old car. (**SUB**)

1. I went to the store before Sushmito arrived.

2. It rained all night, so the tournament was postponed.

3. I like to fish even though I don't catch anything most days.

4. Although Melville's *Moby Dick* is a great book, there are some chapters that are slow reading.

5. Professor Pham asked us not only to compare and contrast Melville and Thoreau, but also to use one or more of their works to support our points.

6. As the sun rose over Lake Mead, the water sparkled with dancing white light.

7. Outside the office it was hot and windy, but inside it was cool and quiet.

8. My grandfather used to say, "You're either part of the solution or part of the problem."

9. Rich and Gary, when they saw the long line for tickets, decided to go home and watch the game on television.

10. She disliked the medicine more than I.

PARTS & PATTERNS

1b, Subjects   **Refer to the Handbook, pp. 144.**

For each sentence that follows, underline the complete subject in the main clause.

For example: <u>Why anybody would live anyplace other than Texas</u> was a mystery to Annie.

1. Because my bearded collie, Kado, sleeps so much, my roommate thinks my dog is a stuffed animal.

2. Ly's enthusiasm for our annual reunion is infectious.

3. Joan's track and swimming talents earned her a scholarship.

4. Calculus 201 and Chemistry 137 have kept me extremely busy this semester.

5. The last time I checked, the university had five libraries.

6. Riding the noisy IRT express train to school ensures that I am completely awake by the time I get off at 116th Street.

7. Branagh's remakes of *Henry V* and *Much Ado About Nothing* have brought Shakespeare to new audiences.

8. There are many ways to define success.

9. Due to record rainfall, the Mississippi River and its many tributaries rose to record levels in 1993.

10. The debate over national health care has raised many difficult questions.

PARTS & PATTERNS

1b, Predicates   **Refer to the Handbook, pp. 145.**

Underline the complete predicate in the main clause of each of the following sentences.

For example: I <u>work in Enrico's Deli from 8 to 11 weeknights.</u>

1. Smoking is expensive and addictive.

2. Juan believed that his studies were a worthwhile investment.

3. Melissa's research paper explored the differences between personal debt and the national debt.

4. Gwen is the oldest of five children.

5. After working together all day, Bill and Ted cooked dinner together also.

6. Cronston Avenue ends just beyond Avenue M.

7. Lions sleep during much of the day.

8. Raoulito was happy he had backed up his hard disk when it crashed only a day later.

9. Nevin was shocked to find it harder to get a driver's license than purchase a gun.

10. Though Eliza lived on the sixth floor, she created a garden of tomatoes, lettuce, onions, and herbs by planting seeds in window boxes.

PARTS & PATTERNS

1b, Objects   **Refer to the Handbook, pp. 145.**

In the following sentences, underline the object(s), and then indicate whether it is a direct object (DO) or an indirect object (IO).

For example: Sally gave <u>me</u> <u>a new book</u> for my birthday.

           IO   *DO*

1. Jerry washed his dog after it fought with a skunk.

2. My grandson brought me flowers for Mother's Day.

3. Iris informed her students about the upcoming exam.

4. The student asked for a better grade on her paper.

5. Julia asked me to take her to the mall.

6. You should take responsibility for your actions.

7. The children offered the teacher candy at the class party.

8. He flattered her with many compliments.

9. Jerry mastered karate.

10. He planned a surprise party for her.

PARTS & PATTERNS

1c, Prepositional Phrases.   **Refer to the Handbook, pp. 146.**

In the following sentences, place parentheses ( ) around the prepositional phrase(s).

For example: She was running with her dog.

          She was running (with her dog.)

1. The rabbit went into its cage.

2. Manuel was scared about entering his new school.

3. The stain on her shirt embarrassed Abigail.

4. The car with the dent on the front fender is my sister's.

5. Running laps around the block became boring for the track star.

6. Have you seen my books in my bedroom?

7. The books on the table have disappeared.

8. I never guessed that the cat would be hiding in the closet in the hallway.

9. In the future, I would like to see you spend more time working on your writing skills.

10. The dog ran to his dish, ate his food quickly, and ran to get his toys.

PARTS & PATTERNS

1c, Verbals   **Refer to the Handbook, pp. 146–147.**

In the following sentences, underline the verbals and verbal phrases. Then identify their type as gerund (GER), infinitive (INF), past participle (PAST PART), or present participle (PRES PART).

For example: <u>Comparing Fred Astaire and Michael Jackson as dancers and singers</u> would be interesting. (**PRES PART**)

1. I love running because it requires so little equipment.

2. Pacing yourself during an exam is crucial.

3. The drummer playing the steel drums is my cousin.

4. The Continental Army, faced with many hardships, managed to defeat the better trained and equipped British.

5. To conduct good science requires first, good training; second, good insight; and third, great effort.

6. Shooting the jumper in basketball is a lot easier when you plant both feet firmly before leaping.

7. The bird singing in the top of that oak tree is a wood thrush.

8. My grandmother always urged me to believe in myself.

9. Feeling the wind come up suddenly, Maggie suspected that a thunderstorm was approaching.

10. Stretching out before running is increasingly important as you age, especially to prevent injuries.

PARTS & PATTERNS

1d, Clauses   **Refer to the Handbook, pp. 147–149.**

Underline and label the adjective (relative) clauses (ADJ CLS), adverb clauses (ADV CLS), and noun clauses (NOUN CLS) in the following sentences.

For example: The fish <u>that live in our lake</u> have been reduced in number recently by an increase in the cormorant population. (**ADJ CLS**)

1. When I saw Roger, who was just returning from a trip, he told me he would be playing softball with us this Saturday.

2. Ceilia painted her house purple because it was her favorite color.

3. If you hit or tip a ball foul and you already have two strikes, the count remains unchanged.

4. He hoped his contribution to the charity would benefit whoever was most in need.

5. After losing three games straight, the team was ecstatic when it beat the undefeated first place team.

6. At the party on the night before she left for college, everyone wished Sumru well.

7. My motorcycle was magnificent when it ran but a great frustration the rest of the time.

8. Milo's family came over after they finished their dinner.

9. He knew a good deal when he saw it.

10. Our school's library, which was built in 1883, is a fine example of H. H. Richardson's work

PARTS & PATTERNS

1e, Types of Sentences   **Refer to the Handbook, pp. 149–150.**

Classify each of the following sentences by type: simple, compound, complex, or compound-complex.

For example: I reeled the fish in, and Bill netted it. (**compound**)

1. Though ordinary ink may look black, it also contains red pigment.

2. Fred likes to read in bed.

3. *The Grapes of Wrath* and *Of Mice and Men* are examples of books read more often in high school than college.

4. After scooping ice cream all summer, my right arm was so strong that I could beat my older brother in arm wrestling, and my left arm looked so withered to me that it seemed almost like the forelegs of *Tyrannosaurus rex*.

5. Though it may sound odd, I swim in the winter and ski in the summer.

6. I read the book and wrote my analysis all in one day.

7. Antonia went from meeting to meeting until three o'clock, and then she caught a cab to the airport for her four o'clock flight.

8. She saved her money until she had enough to buy a laptop computer.

9. I repainted our room before my roommate returned from spring break, and all he could say when he saw it was that I must be color-blind.

10. Though there is much strife in the world, I maintain my optimism because I do not believe in classifying people into separate groups.

PARTS & PATTERNS

2, Subject-Verb Agreement 1   **Refer to the Handbook, pp. 150–155.**

Correct the errors in subject-verb agreement in the following sentences.

For example: The depth of all three ponds are unknown.

Correction: **The depth of all three ponds is unknown.**

1. The ticket, including dinner with dessert, a floor show, and dancing after, cost only twenty dollars.

2. The smell of the ripening apples and pears attract bees to the orchard.

3. Neither my parents nor my brother want to try my latest culinary triumph: cranberry-tofu meat loaf.

4. The democratic minority makes their voices heard.

5. High tides and wind creates dangerous conditions along the coast.

6. Fourteen aunts, uncles, and cousins, except for Gramma Gump, was coming to our cookout.

7. The new library, though it had no windows, were bright and pleasant inside.

8. Six loaves of bread is not enough for this group.

9. The attorney at the offices have been practicing law for fifty years.

10. The House of Representatives are on summer recess.

PARTS & PATTERNS

2e–l, Subject-Verb Agreement 2   **Refer to the Handbook, pp. 153–155.**

Correct the errors in subject-verb agreement in the following sentences.

For example: He was the first of the thirteen batters who was struck out by Clemens.

Correction: He was the first of the thirteen batters who were struck out
                by Clemens.

1. Anyone who study regularly will do better in school and enjoy it more.

2. All the explanations is inadequate.

3. None of my classes meet before 10 a.m.

4. There is, on a regulation baseball team, nine players.

5. Politics both fascinate and repulse him.

6. Newspapers that covers controversial issues must work hard to be fair.

7. *Profiles in Courage* were written by John F. Kennedy.

8. One of his pairs of pants are ripped.

9. Whether privatization will result in more efficient services are debatable.

10. *Data* are the plural of *datum*.

PARTS & PATTERNS

3a–b, Principal Parts of Irregular Verbs

Refer to the Handbook, pp. 156–159.

Correct the misuse of irregular verbs in the following sentences.

For example: When the thunderstorm came through, it awakened me.

Correction: When the thunderstorm came through, it awoke me.

1. If you bent the pipe more, I think it will fit.

2. After John set down, he pulled out a book and dozed off.

3. Having took the subway for years, I was not easily surprised by unusual looking passengers.

4. Paul took the dinner roast out at noon because it was froze.

5. I seen that new movie with Jennifer Lopez last week.

6. I had wrote to him all summer, but he only replied with a single postcard.

7. When the bell rung, the lecturer began immediately.

8. Once the paintings were hanged, the artist relaxed and got ready for the opening.

9. Many flowers and wreaths are lain at the Vietnam Memorial every day.

10. It was his favorite sweatshirt, so he wore it even though it was tore.

PARTS & PATTERNS

3c, Verb Tense   **Refer to the Handbook, pp. 159–161.**

Rewrite the sentence provided in the verb tenses indicated.

For example: John and I often go to the movies together.

Present Perfect: John and I have often gone to the movies together.

I go to the All-Star Game every year.

1. Present Perfect:

2. Present Progressive:

3. Present Perfect Progressive:

4. Past:

5. Past Perfect:

6. Past Progressive:

7. Past Perfect Progressive:

8. Future:

9. Future Perfect:

10. Future Progressive:

11. Future Perfect Progressive:

PARTS & PATTERNS

3e, Verb Mood   **Refer to the Handbook, pp. 163–164.**

Write, in the parentheses provided, the mood of the underlined clause.

For example:

      (   )   <u>Come home after practice</u>.

      (imperative)   <u>Come home after practice</u>.

1. (   )   Bob asked <u>that Joe come early today</u>.

2. (   )   <u>If I were training harder</u>, I would be better prepared.

3. (   )   <u>Every night he reads until bedtime</u>.

4. (   )   Mary said, "<u>Hurry up, or we'll miss the bus</u>."

5. (   )   <u>I wished it were snowing</u>, but it was only raining.

6. (   )   Lili said <u>her voice was similar to Sheryl Crow's</u>.

7. (   )   Don asked <u>if the campers could settle down</u>.

8. (   )   Chris wished <u>he were able to work more than ten hours a week</u>.

9. (   )   <u>If it were up to me</u>, I'd change the policy.

10. (   )   "Don't forget to pick me up, Brutus!"

PARTS & PATTERNS

3f, Active and Passive Voices   **Refer to the Handbook, pp. 164.**

Rewrite each sentence, changing its voice (that is, rewrite sentences in the passive voice to the active voice, and vice versa). Indicate the voice used in your rewritten sentence.

Example: *Star Trek* is loved by millions of Trekkies.

Rewritten: (active) Millions of Trekkies love Star Trek.

1. Jamal mailed the letters after lunch.

2. The dinner was cooked by Raoul.

3. Wallace Stegner wrote *Angle of Repose*.

4. Regina saw the Blue Line bus.

5. The World Series is watched by many people who rarely watch baseball otherwise.

6. The hills were set aglow by the summer sun.

7. Horseback riding demands coordination and skill.

8. Our guide called the tallest redwood the "Mother of the Forest."

9. Their farm produces many gallons of milk each day.

10. In-line skates are often used by people in the park.

PARTS & PATTERNS

4a, Pronoun Agreement
Refer to the Handbook, pp. 165–167.

Correct the errors in pronoun-antecedent agreement in the following sentences.

For example: If someone calls, please tell them I'll call back in an hour.

The problem: *someone* is singular, *them* is plural. There are many possible solutions; here are two:

> If someone calls, please tell him or her I'll call back in an hour.

> (grammatically correct but somewhat awkward)

> If someone calls, please say I'll call back in an hour.

> (switch to the verb *say*, which doesn't require an indirect object such as *them, him,* or *her.*)

1. The jury provided their decision to the judge.

2. He needs to better train his dog Biff, which barks at the letter carrier every day.

3. Neither of the girls can baby-sit their little sister.

4. When Louisa and Hal come to visit, they always bring his and her dog.

5. Each player in the tournament took their turn at the table.

6. The orchestra will open their twenty-eighth season with tonight's performance.

7. Either you or your sister need to mow the lawn today.

8. Nicole's brother, which served in the Navy, is going to marry my sister.

9. A doctor needs to be calm when talking to their patients

10. If someone liked *E.T.*, they will love *A.I.*

PARTS & PATTERNS

4b, Pronoun Reference   **Refer to the Handbook, pp. 167–169.**

Correct the vague or confusing pronoun references in the following sentences.

For example: Lisa told Joan that her car sounded as though it needed a tune up.

The problem: Whose car needs a tune up, Lisa's or Joan's? There are many possible solutions; here is one:

Lisa said, "Joan, your car sounds as though it needs a tune up."

1. I'm concerned about that.

2. Professor Tecknor, who studies psychology and relationships, gave a lecture on it at our seminar.

3. Though I know that supply-side economics focuses on production, and demand-side economics emphasizes consumption, this has never helped me understand where my paycheck goes every week.

4. When the company demanded a cut in wages and benefits, they recommended a strike vote be taken.

5. When tours come through our town, they often stop at the Shelburne Museum, where you can see an extensive American folk art collection.

6. Santa Cruz County offers both the mountains and the ocean, so they rarely wish to move anywhere else.

7. The freeway was backed up all the way to the toll plaza, and it was unlikely to clear out for several hours.

8. Cormac McCarthy's *All the Pretty Horses* combines ample description with sparse dialog, and it creates a sense of the lone horseman riding through the vast, southwestern landscape.

9. In the newspaper they reported the show opens tomorrow.

10. Driving into Livonia on my last trip, which is near Detroit, I ran out of gas.

PARTS & PATTERNS

4c, Pronoun Case 1   **Refer to the Handbook, pp. 169–172.**

Correct the pronoun case errors in the following sentences.

For example: The woman on the right is her.

Correction: **The woman on the right is she.**

1. Have you seen mine brother?

2. After taking the train, Chuck and me went to the deli.

3. If it were up to Laura and I, we'd leave now.

4. The boss appreciated them working on Saturday night.

5. My sister said she would be going to visit our grandmother after visiting Susan and I.

6. The choice for employee of the week is between you and I.

7. Us winning the Tri-City Invitational made the whole school proud.

8. Her and me studied for the exam with Tom, Rico, and Zino.

9. The president of the student council is him.

10. Because the package was addressed to she and I, we did not wait for my brother to get home before opening it.

PARTS & PATTERNS

4c–d, Pronoun Case 2   **Refer to the Handbook, pp. 169–173.**

Correct the pronoun case errors in the following sentences.

For example: Fritz likes to swim more than me.

Correction: Fritz likes to swim more than I.

1. Professor Malcolm asked Dave and I to participate in the experiment.

2. Despite all his campaigning, the incumbent was running stronger than him, as the *New York Times* reported.

3. My sister, whom has incredibly acute hearing when it comes to the telephone, yelled out from the shower, "Who is that call for?"

4. Our best hitter came to the plate with two runners on, Lana and I.

5. The victory will go to whoever wins.

6. The registrar required Donna and she to submit transcripts for their summer work.

7. My brother and I are avid readers, but he hasn't read as many books as me this summer.

8. Because it was a tie, the prize was given to two runners, Phil and I.

9. I forget her name, but the Oscar for Best Actress went to whomever played the older sister in *Howard's End.*

10. *For Whom the Bell Tolls* was written by who?

PARTS & PATTERNS

5, Adjectives and Adverbs   **Refer to the Handbook, pp. 173–177.**

Correct the errors in adjective and adverb usage in the following sentences.

For example: Josh can swim real fast.

Correction: Josh can swim really fast.

1. Laura grew more and more confidently as the semester progressed.

2. I think it's coldest today than yesterday.

3. The CIA is charged with monitoring this kind of sensitive security issues.

4. He is doing good in pottery class.

5. With two of their starters on the disabled list, things look badly for the Seattle Mariners.

6. The steadily increase in sales before the holidays was offset by their declining steadily for the six months after the holidays.

7. After eating a $9 Tub-o-Pop at the movies, Sam was feeling badly.

8. Dirk read so quick that he finished the assignment a day before me.

9. The actors sure surprised me with their performance.

10. Even though Elaine was a healthy thirty-four-year-old who had always eaten good, each Thanksgiving her grandmother said she looked a little thin.

PARTS & PATTERNS

6, Sentence Fragments 1   **Refer to the Handbook, pp. 177–181.**

For each of the following entries, indicate whether it is a fragment (F) or a complete sentence (S). Your answer may refer to part of the entry or the entire entry. If the entry is a fragment, change it so it is a complete sentence.

Example: Especially because she was a wonderful speller.

Answer: F; She wrote well because she was a wonderful speller.

1. Rhonda ran to the store. Because she needed milk.

2. The big, black dog prancing down the crowded sidewalk.

3. As long as you support your point.

4.   We are having a party tonight after our class and work.

5. The cat that climbed the tree. It is a stray.

6. To play for a professional hockey team and then to be a hockey coach.

7. The winning team celebrated on the field.

8. You have to do the laundry. Before you go to work.

9. Driving while talking on a cell phone. Terrence had an accident.

10. It soon became apparent. That the group was not working well together.

PARTS & PATTERNS

6, Sentence Fragments 2   **Refer to the Handbook, pp. 177–181.**

Rewrite the following sentences to eliminate sentence fragments.

For example: He loves to fish. Also hunt and hike.

Correction: He loves to fish, hunt, and hike.

1. My little brother is 6' 2." And still growing.

2. My big brother Todd likes to dance. Especially to hip-hop music.

3. While on vacation I read two books. Nicholas Evans's *The Horse Whisperer* and Frances Mayes's *Under the Tuscan Sun.*

4. Last night I saw Neville at the student union; Molly, too.

5. When I saw the *Mona Lisa* in person. I was, to be honest, disappointed.

6. The city's jobs bill was stalled in the state legislature. Which is unfortunate.

7. Writing a good essay is time consuming. But is necessary to pass the class.

8. I saw most of my family over Thanksgiving. Anne, Michael, Kate, and Maggie.

9. Gertrude is my closest friend. Even though she moved to Poland.

10. After summer, I saw Jean very little. By winter, not at all.

PARTS & PATTERNS

7, Comma Splices 1   **Refer to the Handbook, pp. 181–184.**

Rewrite the following sentences to eliminate comma splices, using a different method to correct each sentence.

For example: I love to cook, I hate to diet.

Correction: I love to cook, but hate to diet.

Correction: Although I love to cook, I hate to diet.

Correction: I love to cook; I hate to diet.

Correction: I love to cook. I hate to diet.

1. Margaret is getting married on Saturday, I hope it doesn't rain then.

2. Professor Gerson has a pleasantly acid sense of humor, he quipped that the term *European ally* is an oxymoron.

3. I practice piano one hour every day, this has helped me improve a lot in the last year.

4. Spring in San Francisco is cool, many visitors wished they had brought warmer clothes.

5. I am a business major, studying economics will give me a useful background.

6. Picasso's work has been classified into periods, perhaps best known is his Blue Period.

7. It was raining lightly, we set off on the hike anyway.

8. My roommate reported that my old sneakers had begun to move on their own, he said they were a violation of U.S. treaties banning the development of biological weapons.

9. I had never driven to San Jose before, I missed my exit from Route 85.

10. Kaitlin reads the newspaper every morning, she is much more knowledgeable about current affairs than I.

PARTS & PATTERNS

7, Comma Splices 2   **Refer to the Handbook, pp. 181–184.**

Rewrite the following sentences to eliminate comma splices, using a different method to correct each sentence.

For example: I love to cook, I hate to diet.

Correction: I love to cook, but hate to diet.

Correction: Although I love to cook, I hate to diet.

Correction: I love to cook; I hate to diet.

Correction: I love to cook. I hate to diet.

1. The days are beginning to get longer, there's more sun every day.

2. With all the channel choices on cable and satellite TV these days, I wish there was something good to watch, it seems like there were better programs when I had fewer choices.

3. Can you read this, I don't have my glasses with me.

4. They weren't important ideas, they were interesting suggestions.

5. I didn't know what I wanted to study in college, I had too many choices, and I felt confused.

6. He enjoys skiing, hiking, and fishing, he often tries to participate in all three activities in one day.

7. When I play video games, I like to pretend I am involved in the action, it helps me imagine the next move.

8. *Good* is not a very specific word, some other words are more descriptive.

9. The carpenter finished his work on the building, the electrician needed more time, the bricklayer was late, the painter waited patiently for all of them.

10. She said, "I don't understand the question, what do you mean?"

PARTS AND PATTERNS

7, Run-on Sentences 1   **Refer to the Handbook, pp. 181–184.**

Rewrite the following to eliminate fused or run-on sentences.

For example: Mariah was very physically fit she worked out five days a week.

Correction: Mariah was very physically fit because she worked out five days a week.

1. We took a cab to the theatre we saw *Rent*

2. I hope Ben will come over and help me with my car I need to adjust the carburetor.

3. It rained for twenty days straight I felt like escaping to the desert.

4. I know what an armadillo looks like I'm not quite sure what an aardvark looks like.

5. The last U.S. space shuttle flight to *Mir* was made in 1999, since then all shuttle flights have been to the new International Space Station.

6. I saw Leah yesterday she looked great.

7. I think it's three o'clock do we have to leave now?

8. When I visited Maria over the holidays, I met many of her high school friends they were very friendly.

9. Can you come here and taste this soup I need an opinion.

10. We trained the telescope to the south Saturn was clearly visible.

PARTS AND PATTERNS

7, Run-On Sentences 2   **Refer to the Handbook, pp. 181–184.**

Rewrite the following to eliminate fused or run-on sentences.

For example: Tony likes all music his favorite is hip hop.

Correction: Tony likes all music, but his favorite is hip hop.

1. The audience cheered the actors bowed.

2. The guitarist was excellent the girl sang well, too.

3. Janel got an A on her essay she must have written many drafts.

4. By then, the baby was asleep the mother was too tired to cook.

5. In the waiting room, a man was reading a book a woman was watching TV.

6. Shawn mowed the lawn then he raked the grass.

7. Cedric ran the laps until he was exhausted he sat on the bleachers to catch his breath.

8. Fish make great pets they require little care.

9. Did you know fish play with one another they chase each other around the fish tank.

10. The class seemed to last forever the instructor lectured for two hours.

VII   PUNCTUATION

1a–c, The Comma 1   Refer to the Handbook, pp. 185–188.

In the following sentences, correct the comma errors by adding or removing commas.

For example: I limbered up for twenty minutes and I went for a five-mile run.

Correction: I limbered up for twenty minutes, and I went for a five-mile run.

1. He worked hard yet he was not feeling tired.

2. As Felix watched the cat ate her breakfast of Tuna Delight.

3. Last semester I had Professor Roop for history which has always been my favorite subject.

4. Yawning Marlena put down her book and went to bed.

5. My oldest brother Geoffrey usually comes for Thanksgiving.

6. Ben's favorite book *Animal Farm,* was written by George Orwell.

7. Although I get up very early in the summer I am able to sleep later during the winter.

8. Driving in the Indianapolis 500 which is one of America's premier races, was an immense thrill for Sharleen.

9. Taken together hot weather and no increase in electrical supply cause even more widespread rolling blackouts.

10. Having gotten lost twice already Doug thought it would be wise to ask for directions at the service station.

PUNCT

1d–g, The Comma 2

Refer to the Handbook, pp. 188–190.

In the following sentences, correct the comma errors by adding or removing commas.

For example: I need to go to the bookstore, the library and the registrar's.

Correction: I need to go to the bookstore, the library, and the registrar's.

1. The recipe specifically called for three, large, red tomatoes.

2. This fall Eliot was reading Ernest Hemingway, Maya Angelou and Alice Walker.

3. For this reason the committee voted to change the policy.

4. President Jimmy Carter may turn out to be more effective out of office than in unlike Lyndon Johnson.

5. Riding into a headwind, can help you improve your cycling endurance, power and technique.

6. John was elected by his peers to lead the team, and therefore feels both honored and pressured.

7. The cost of health care has increased for example at a rate that far outstrips inflation.

8. As the workweek has been shortened, productivity has increased not decreased.

9. Their new house on Willow Street is small square and energy efficient.

10. They will discover however that not doing their homework will result in more difficulty with their tests.

PUNCT

1h–l, The Comma 3   **Refer to the Handbook, pp. 190–192.**

Correct the errors by adding commas in the following sentences.

For example: The enthusiastic audience called out "More! More!"

Correction: The enthusiastic audience called out, "More! More!"

1. I smiled and said "Yes I'll be there."

2. If you want to call Jessica has a phone.

3. Our reservations are for Friday October 26 through Sunday November 11.

4. Luke called yesterday and said "Congratulations on your new baby."

5. Lonnie gave me a ride from Tulsa Oklahoma to Paris Texas.

6. After dinner check the answering machine for messages.

7. John is drinking water and Mary prefers soda.

8. "Well please come in" said my father graciously.

9. The senator's aides said their office had received more than 1400 letters in favor of the bill.

10. After Celia graduates, she will be known as Celia Barnes MD emergency doctor.

PUNCT

1m, The Comma 4 Refer to the Handbook, pp. 192–193.

Correct the following sentences by removing unnecessary commas.

For example: Maybe, you'll receive the letter today.

Correction: Maybe you'll receive the letter today.

1. Adela and her brother, watched *Lost,* every week.

2. I drove, last week, to Pullman, Washington, to visit my best friends.

3. Reviewers are critical of comedies, like, *Two and a Half Men.*

4. If I, were you, I would leave before rush hour.

5. The small, gold, locket was a family heirloom.

6. He shipped me a box, that contained four hundred yo-yo's, missing strings.

7. He liked music by groups such as, A Tribe Called Quest, Massive Attack, and The Brand New Heavies.

8. Jobs, jobs, and jobs, was the theme of his campaign.

9. He came early, and left late, much to my surprise.

10. She loved to go to the museum, on Saturday, but he, preferred Sunday.

PUNCT

2, The Semicolon   **Refer to the Handbook, pp. 193–195.**

Correct the following sentences by either adding or removing semicolons as appropriate. Some sentences may be correct as given.

For example: It was a cool, gray day, the beach was empty.

Correction: It was a cool, gray day; the beach was empty.

1. The drive from Akron to Cincinnati was long; but I didn't mind; nor did my sister.

2. The rapid decrease in computer hardware prices has put pressure on software developers to do the same, nonetheless, they have resisted the trend for the most part.

3. On one recent weekend I saw *Pearl Harbor*, which used extensive computer-generated simulations of an historical event, *The Matrix*, which explored virtual worlds accessed via mind control, and *Until the End of the World*, which presented computer-driven dream exploration.

4. I was shocked when I drove the $20,000 car, it rode only a bit better than my current car, which has a book value of only $1,500.

5. Although I support universal access to health care; I disagree with combining it with a flat rate; providing access shouldn't eliminate government support entirely.

6. He was my best friend; and because of this, he was always welcome in my family's home.

7. My family took a raft trip down the Colorado River; which is rated 9 of a possible 10 in terms of difficulty.

8. We thought we'd visit John on the way; but we ran out of time and had to pass by without stopping.

9. My sister's letter from Yellowstone National Park in Wyoming took fourteen days to reach me, the letter and the park she described were both full of wonders.

10. The rainfall for the month of August was only four inches, however, that was normal for the region.

PUNCT

3, The Colon   **Refer to the Handbook, pp. 195–197.**

Correct the following sentences by either adding or removing colons as appropriate. Some sentences may be correct as given. Remember that sometimes a colon can take the place of other punctuation.

For example: Allan counted up his Halloween catch; thirty-eight candy bars, seven different types of chewing gum, and miscellaneous fruit that he did not even bother to count.

Correction: Allan counted up his Halloween catch: thirty-eight candy bars, seven different types of chewing gum, and miscellaneous fruit that he did not even bother to count.

1. I have passed along to my children one of my father's sayings, "When you borrow something, try to return it in better condition than you received it."

2. Scientists, in an effort to isolate what it is in food that makes most people evaluate it as "tasting good or delicious," have determined the single most important ingredient, fat.

3. On your way home please pick up: a pound of cold cuts, a head of lettuce, and a video.

4. Today is a very good day for haying; plenty of sunshine, a light breeze, and low humidity.

5. We took the following route, Route 80 to Rock Springs, Route 187 to Farson, and Route 28 to South Pass City.

6. He speaks four languages, English, French, German, and Spanish.

7. Many vegetarians have a curious blind spot. They don't seem to realize that plants are just as alive as animals.

8. Professor Thomason argued that there was one reason the United States had not acted more decisively in Bosnia, it has no oil.

9. My aunt is fond of quoting from the Bible and regularly recites Luke 1, 2.

10. The Great Lakes include: Huron, Ontario, Michigan, Erie, and Superior.

PUNCT

4, The Apostrophe   **Refer to the Handbook, pp. 197–200.**

Correct the following sentences by either adding or removing apostrophes as appropriate.

For example: Do you know the origin of the expression "Mind your ps and qs"?

Correction: Do you know the origin of the expression "Mind your p's and q's"?

1. Did you see the film *My Mothers Castle?*

2. My grandmother told me that the 38 hurricane was much worse than this years storm.

3. A snake sheds it's skin when its growing.

4. What is our companys policy regarding maternity leave?

5. I thought it was her's, but perhaps its really Bills.

6. I really enjoyed E. L. Doctorows novel *World's Fair.*

7. Jon's and Emily's dog, Bumper, has knocked over our garbage again. Now I know why thats his' name.

8. He accepted the Chief's of Staff recommendation.

9. Until this semester I had never used Petersens's Theory.

10. The teachers union and our school board seemed forever in negotiation.

PUNCT

5, Quotation Marks   **Refer to the Handbook, pp. 200–203.**

Correct the following sentences by either adding, altering, or removing quotation marks and related punctuation as appropriate.

For example: O. Henry's short story The Gift of the Magi was included in his first book of stories, "The Four Million."

Correction: O. Henry's short story **"The Gift of the Magi"** was included in his first book of stories, *The Four Million.*

1. "Where you place your commas is one of my teacher's "pet peeves", so I always double check my work", said Elaine.

2. "Would you like to come to dinner with us"? Mary asked.

3. When I read computer magazines I find all the technobabble confusing: "RAM," "ROM" and "bytes." Who dreams up these terms?

4. Milan told me that "Faulkner wrote the novel 'As I Lay Dying' in only six weeks."

5.   "I hope you'll come to our party tonight, said Alison.

     "Me too, I replied. "but I have to work until 11."

     "That's no problem; she said. It doesn't even start until 10, and I doubt you'll miss anything. Just come as you are after work.

6. Last year when I reread the book, "*To Kill a Mockingbird*", I discovered it was much more interesting than I ever remembered it to be.

7. Ryan's chapter for his book, The Changing Status of Euthanasia in the United States, helped him clinch a "great" rating on the best seller list.

8. Lawrence had mixed feelings about hearing the president quoting from the Eagles' song Take It to the Limit. Was this the movie "The Big Chill" come to life?

9. The proceeds go to a worthy cause, the "Jaime. L. Barzenté Memorial Fund."

10. "Where's the power switch,"? said Tom, as smoke poured from his computer.

PUNCT

6a, The Period   **Refer to the Handbook, pp. 203–204.**

Correct the errors in the use of the period in the following sentences.

For example: Dorothy asked me if I was aware that sit-ups could strain my back?

Correction: Dorothy asked me if I was aware that sit-ups could strain my back.

1. If you know the Latin meaning abbreviated by am and pm, you will find it easier to remember which one to use.

2. One of the experimental drugs being used to combat AIDS is A.Z.T.

3. I wondered if he knew what the U.S.D.A. stamp on the meat stood for.

4. One of the most woeful scenes in all of Shakespeare is in *King Lear*

5. Tintin's best friend is Capt Horatio Haddock.

6. Last December he was promoted to president at Kahrdif, Inc..

7. Has your teacher ever told you to avoid using *etc* in your writing?

8. When Bert graduates from medical school next month, he will be Dr Umberto Baldi.

9. They live just off South Main St, I think.

10. Jerry asked me what time I had arrived at work this morning?

PUNCT

6b–c. The Question Mark and Exclamation Point   Refer to the Handbook, pp. 205.

Correct the errors in the use of the question mark and exclamation point in the following sentences.

For example: When is he coming.

Correction: When is he coming**?**

1. Joyce said, "Do you know whether bus or subway is the better way to get to Avenue J from here."

2. As usual for this region, the weather was sunny!

3. Which route to Des Moines has less traffic, John wanted to know?

4. "Can I come too," my sister asked.

5. Louis asked me which class I liked best?

6. Rolf asked me, "What is the difference between a CD and CD-ROM."

7. Wow. This pie is fabulous.

8. Whose book is that.

9. "Is that your book," Lisa asked me?

10. I could not remember when they were coming?

PUNCT

6d–h, Other Punctuation   **Refer to the Handbook, pp. 206–210.**

Correct the punctuation errors involving the use of the dash, period, question mark, exclamation point, parentheses, brackets, ellipses, and the slash in the following sentences.

For example: Batman and Robin; also known as the "dynamic duo"; have been popular with three generations.

Correction: Batman and Robin—also known as the "dynamic duo"—have been popular with three generations. OR
Batman and Robin, also known as the "dynamic duo," have been popular with three generations.

1. One awkward, but acceptable, solution to the problem of sexism in pronouns is the use of *him*, *her* as well as *he or she*.

2. When in Rome (as the saying goes) do as the Romans do.

3. In her research paper, Elizabeth quoted Sam Jones, "The incidence of Alzheimer's increases with ages, sic, and more with women than men."

4. "Our class meets in that new science building. What's its name? Something Hall ... . Burstein ... . Gurstein? I can't remember," said John.

5. I still remember the opening lines of Shakespeare's Sonnet LXXIII:

   "That time of year thou mayst in me behold When yellow leaves, or none, or few, do hang

   Upon those boughs which shake against the cold."

6. Leave now? We just got here—

7. The Reds' starting pitcher, my neighbor's son, Jason, wound up and delivered an 80 mph fastball.

8. I was happy I had voted for him, until he actually won the election.

9. The lecture, a ninety-minute torrent of anecdotes, facts, figures, and numerous slides, left me exhilarated but exhausted.

10. John fed his horses alfalfa, hay, oats, etc.. Too often it caused colic.

VIII MECHANICS

MECH

1a–d, Capitals 1   **Refer to the Handbook, pp. 211–214.**

Correct the errors in capitalization in the following sentences.

For example: Last Fall we hiked in the grand canyon.

Correction: Last fall we hiked in the Grand Canyon.

1. Unfortunately, stargazers living this far South can't see the north star.

2. When James "joe" Jackson sang last week at the hartford ave grill, the crowd roared its approval.

3. The Cold War may be over, but we're still paying the bill.

4. The baptist church in my town sponsors a Community food bank.

5. In the last four months, the missouri and mississippi rivers reached record flood levels, but the hudson river was below normal.

6. I sat late into the night with my family to see Neil Armstrong walk on the moon on july 20, 1969, during the *apollo 11* mission.

7. Last quarter, the Ford and Chrysler Companies reported increased sales, while at General Motors Corporation sales were flat.

8. My cousin Louise is the Founder of the organization, sahm, stay at home moms.

9. Once labor day weekend rolls around, you know that Summer is really over.

10. My Mother is a protestant, and my Father, a muslim.

MECH

1e–j, Capitals 2   **Refer to the Handbook, pp. 214–216.**

Correct the errors in capitalization in the following sentences.

For example: When the storm came through, the weather turned cold. no, it became bitter.

Correction: When the storm came through, the weather turned cold. No, it became bitter.

1. In a recent article, commentator Julia Webb wrote, "for the first time in U.S. history, by the year 2002, more than 50 percent of all American jobs will require at least one year of college."

2. I read the *daily plains record* every day to keep up on local news.

3. During the Spring Semester, Dennis is going to enroll in Calculus, History, and English.

4. I think she bought one of the new Apple Notebook Computers.

5. Who reports on the News Media? the News Media do.

6. Have you read Tom Wolfe's *the bonfire of the vanities?*

7. Our city has two Mosques, four Temples, and twenty-eight Churches of various denominations.

8. Ford Trucks outsell all other makes in new england.

9. During my first Semester at the university of Arizona, I was swamped with work but very happy.

10. In what year did Fitzgerald write *the great gatsby?*

MECH

2, Abbreviations   **Refer to the Handbook, pp. 216–218.**

Correct the errors in the use of abbreviations in the following sentences.

For example: Laura's commission on new sales was 8 pct.

Correction: Laura's commission on new sales was 8 percent.

1. He reported to Sgt. Bilko.

2. The president announced that the new policy was designed to protect our natl. security.

3. Aristotle was born in B.C. 384.

4. Dr. C. Everett Koop, M.D. gave the keynote address.

5. For the trip, they packed clothes, food, games, and etc.

6. The dissolution of the Soviet Union has generated much debate over the future of N.A.T.O.

7. If we leave now, we'll get home in the p.m.

8. After completing her course work, Samantha was awarded a bachelor's degree in psych.

9. Do you know the topic of Prof. Montrose's lecture for our 9 am seminar?

10. British & American English differ in many small ways; e.g., we place a period after the
abbreviation for *Mister* (Mr.), whereas the British do not.

MECH

3, Numbers

Refer to the Handbook, pp. 218–220.

Correct the errors in the use of numbers in the following sentences.

For example: Devon was born in nineteen seventy-one.

Correction: **Devon was born in 1971.**

1. Armand cut the plank into four six-foot sections.

2. Charles Lindbergh began his historic 2-day flight on May 20th, 1927, from Roosevelt Field, Long Island.

3. Scott thought the boat out to Catalina Island cost more than $20.00.

4. American Airlines currently has over six hundred twenty planes.

5. Over the holidays, we saw four films, two plays, and 13 videos.

6. The competition was very close: only 1/8 of a second separated the 6 sprinters.

7. At the beginning of the 20th century, individuals traveled largely by horse; now we drive cars. What will we be doing at the end of the 21st century?

8. The final score was Tigers eight, Panthers two.

9. Our state budget is over 2,300,000,000 dollars.

10. We got up at seven a.m. and swam before breakfast.

MECH

4, Italics/Underlining   **Refer to the Handbook, pp. 220–223.**

Correct the following sentences by adding or removing italics as appropriate. Remember to indicate italics with continuous underlining (<u>such as this sample</u>).

For example: John told me to check The Cambridge Encyclopedia of Language.

Correction: John told me to check <u>The Cambridge Encyclopedia of Language</u>.

1. Linda likes Microsoft Word, but I prefer WordPerfect.

2. The most commonly occurring word in English is the.

3. I asked him to explain what noblesse oblige means.

4. Did you read last week's cover story in Newsweek?

5. Tina objected to Dickens's frequent use of a deus ex machina to resolve his fantastically-plotted novels.

6. Preston rode the Amtrak Empire Builder from Chicago, Illinois, to Portland, Oregon.

7. James Fenimore Cooper's The Last of the Mohicans was made into a movie 166 years after its original publication.

8. The radio show All Things Considered is considered liberal by conservatives and conservative by liberals; maybe that is how the producers came to name the show.

9. His class is reading Dante's Divine Comedy in parallel texts.

10. Before she left on her cruise, her friends wished her *bon voyage*.

MECH

5, The Hyphen   Refer to the Handbook, pp. 223–226.

Correct the following sentences by either adding or removing hyphens as appropriate.

For example: His one year old car still looked brand-new.

Correction: His one-year-old car still looked brand new.

1. I am very close to my brother in law.

2. The ex Metropolitan Opera soprano joined our community chorus and improved the entire section's performance.

3. Are you looking forward to the beginning of the school-year?

4. Our class voted twenty one to seventeen for more study time.

5. In pre revolutionary America, the colonists were subjects of the king of England.

6. The police officer told me that J walking was illegal in this town.

7. The groom nearly fainted when the best-man couldn't find the wedding ring.

8. The governor elect will face many difficult issues this year.

9. When I was a thirteen year old, I played a lot of base-ball.

10. From the eighteenth- to the twentieth-centuries, the West evolved from a pre industrial society to a post industrial one.

MECH

6a, Basic Spelling Rules   **Refer to the Handbook, pp. 227–230.**

Correct the spelling errors in the following sentences by applying the basic spelling rules.

For example: I beleive that he'll be over by eight o'clock.

Correction: I believe that he'll be over by eight o'clock.

1. I'm hopeing we can see Jeri before she leaves.

2. Professor Guimard is very knowledgable about plate tectonics.

3. Lorraine was lying down thinking when an idea suddenly occured to her; half an hour later she had laid out all the fundamentals in the feild of astronomy.

4. How much did you say you payed for those peachs?

5. I sent the package via Federal Express, so he ought to recieve it by noon tommorrow.

6. No sooner had the city finished paveing our street than the Water Department tore it back up again.

7. I love my brother, but I still think he's wierd.

8. These days, most people don't bother to pick up pennys.

9. It might sound odd, but our paper has two editor-in-chiefs.

10. We spend a lot of time with our nieghbors.

MECH

6b, Words that Sound Alike   **Refer to the Handbook, pp. 231–232.**

The following sentences contain homophones used in error. Replace the incorrect word in each sentence with its correct sound-alike.

For example: After much deliberation, he decided to except their job offer.

Correction: **After much deliberation, he decided to accept their job offer.**

1. When I reached the library, I was gasping for breathe.

2. In the 100-meter finals, Sarah was third and I was forth.

3. My father is sight manager for the new Deeter Building construction project.

4. My teacher recommended that we always read the forward, as it usually defines the scope and approach of the book that follows.

5. All the people I know with personal stationary are of my parents' generation.

6. When the passed president of the AFL-CIO addressed our school, he complemented the White House's new labor relations policy.

7. If their coming with us, they have too hurry up.

8. I would rather work now, finish the reading, and than go to the late show.

9. Whose playing against the Miami Heat tonight?

10. The teenage years can be a period of extreme pier pressure.

IX RESEARCH WRITING

RESEARCH

Research exercises are incorporated into chapter XI, MLA Style Documentation, and Format; chapter XII, APA Style Documentation, and Format; and chapter XIII, CMS Documentation and Format/CSE Documentation.

X   WRITING IN THE DISCIPLINES

1a Understand Your Writing Assignment   Refer to the Handbook, pp. 276–277.

Using the following list of direction words, create a series of questions that will limit and focus the content of your paper. Select only the direction words that apply to the type of assignment. Refer to pp. 276–277 in your handbook for the meanings of the direction words.

Analyze

Argue

Categorize

Compare

Contrast

Critique

Define

Describe

Evaluate

Explain

Identify

Illustrate

Interpret

List

Outline

Prove

Review

Synthesize

Trace

WRIT DISCIPLINES

**1b, e. Methods/Evidence and
Documentation/Format**

Refer to the Handbook, pp. 277–280.

Answer the following questions.

1. Define primary sources and give an example.

2. Define secondary sources and give an example.

3. Discuss the characteristics of an authoritative and reliable Internet source. Give an example of an authoritative and reliable Internet source for your discipline or paper topic.

4. What disciplines use the following documentation styles?

   a. MLA

   b. APA

   c. CMS

   d. CSE

5. What is the common feature of all four of the above mentioned documentation styles?

WRIT DISCIPLINES

2d, Conventions for Writing about Literature   Refer to the Handbook, pp. 283–285.

The following brief piece about Ernest Hemingway's "The Snows of Kilimanjaro" contains a number of violations of the conventions and suggestions contained in WRIT DISCIPLINES 2. Rewrite the piece making appropriate edits, and be prepared to discuss and explain your edits. Use MLA formatting conventions. (See Annotated Student Essay about Literature, pp. 287-289, in your Handbook.)

The Age of Wisdom, The Age of Despair:

Hemingway on Safari

Ernest Hemingway's short story, *The Snows of Kilimanjaro*, was the unhappy story of a man, Harry, on safari with his wife, and dying of an infection resulting from a scratch from a thorn bush received some two weeks before the story opens. The action takes place over a period of two days, during which Harry drinks whiskey-and-soda, sleeps, dreams stories he wishes he had written, and argues with his wife. During the second night of the story, Harry died while dreaming of flying past Mt. Kilimanjaro, Africa's highest peak at 19,710 feet.

The author opens the story by saying:

"The marvelous thing is that it's painless," he said. "That's how you know when it starts."

"Is it really?"

"Absolutely. I'm awfully sorry about the odor though. That must bother you."

"Don't! Please don't."

"Look at them," he said. "Now is it sight or is it scent that brings them like that?"

And so the essay is off and running, with the author dying and his wife, Helen, not at all sure if Hemingway is telling the truth or just keeping a stiff upper lip. Like much of Ernest's short fiction, this novella, collected in "The First Forty-nine," published in 1938 by Scribners and Sons, highlights the tensions between life's inherent drama and the author's preoccupation with separating himself from that drama. Here Harry is dying and he refers to the whole event as pain-free, even as his body is being ravaged by spreading gangrene, and his conversations with his wife are marked by bitterness as he calls her names, all the while never even addressing her by name.

Thus a life-threatening situation, in which most of us would rely heavily upon family, instead finds Hemingway armoring himself with whiskey, distancing himself from his wife, and withdrawing into delusional isolation.

Though Ernest Hemingway was relatively young and famous at the time of writing this story, he comes across as world-weary and aged beyond his years. Hemingway said that his goal was to write the truth; sadly, here we find that the truth is a world of misery.

WRIT DISCIPLINES

2d, 3d, 4d, 5d
Conventions   Refer to the Handbook, pp. 283–285, 292–293, 297–298, 301–302.

Fill in the blanks in the following statements.

All Disciplines

1. Formal research writing in all of the disciplines avoids the _____ and _____ points of view.

Literature

2. When writing about literature, you can assume your readers already have read the piece of literature, so you can avoid _____.

3. When mentioning an author the first time within your paper, use the author's _____. After the first time, use _____.

4. Use the _____ tense when discussing works of literature. Use the _____ tense when referring to historical events, biographical material, or events prior to the time of the story's action.

Humanities

5. Investigators in the humanities rely heavily on _____ investigation in their research.

6. Researchers ask questions in order to _____, _____, or _____.

Social Sciences

7. Social sciences have their own technical language with specific meanings for words such as _____, _____, and _____.

8. Social scientists value _____ language and _____, _____, and _____ sentences in reporting their results.

Natural and Applied Sciences

9. Scientists make an effort to create a _____ or _____ tone, preferring verbs that are _____ rather than _____.

10 . Scientists include only information that enhances the reader's understanding of the _____, _____, and _____ of the experiment being discussed.

CHAPTER XI MLA–STYLE DOCUMENTATION AND FORMAT

MLA

Questions **Refer to the Handbook, chapter XI.**

Respond to the following short answer questions.

1. What do the letters in the abbreviation MLA stand for?

2. What is the two-part system of documentation for MLA?

3. Why are in-text citations used in MLA-style documentation?

4. In most MLA in-text citations, what two elements of the source are included?

5. If you are citing a source with more than one author, how do you present the in-text citation?

6. If you are citing an electronic source, how do you present the in-text citation?

7. What is the list of sources in an MLA-style paper titled?

8. In what order are citations given in the list of sources in an MLA-style paper?

9. What are the formatting features of the list of sources in an MLA-style paper?

10. Describe the manuscript format for an MLA-style paper.

MLA

Avoiding Plagiarism   **Refer to the Handbook chapter IX, pp. 264–266.**

For each of the quotations provided, write an acceptable paraphrase and a paraphrase including a partial quotation that avoids plagiarism. Pay particular attention to the word choice and sentence structure of the original.

1. "America is a throw-away society that discards every year 41 million tons of food and yard waste, 13 million tons of metal, 12 million tons of glass, and 10 million tons of plastic." (after Jim Hightower's *War on Waste*)

   _____

   _____

   _____

   _____

2. "All light sources emit waves uniformly in all directions. The amplitude of the waves is perceived by the eye as brightness, or luminance. In space the light waves from stars travel unimpeded and their self-propagating quality perpetuates them infinitely." (after Jeff Burger's *Desktop Multimedia Bible*)

   _____

   _____

   _____

   _____

   _____

3. "The sperm whale is the largest of the toothed whales. Moby Dick was a sperm whale. Generally, male toothed whales are larger than the females. Female sperm whales may grow 35 to 40 feet in length, while the males may reach 60 feet." (after Richard Hendrick et al.'s *The Voyage of the Mimi*)

_____

_____

_____

_____

_____

4. "The humble Teddy Bear not only launched an industry and increased Teddy Roosevelt's popularity, it also fostered the American tendency to focus on the personality rather than the policies of our political leaders." (after Brier, Rosenzweig, and Brown's *Who Built America?*)

_____

_____

_____

_____

_____

5. "On first inspection, the novels of Hemingway and Fitzgerald seem altogether at odds: Hemingway's abrupt dialog and action-filled story lines have a swagger to them that is a world apart from Fitzgerald's polished conversations and drawing room drama. But beyond these superficial differences, both authors create characters aching to find meaning in the confusing modernity of the early twentieth century." (after Oscar Deep's *Defining the Modern Mind*)

_____

_____

_____

_____

6. "Astronauts from over twenty nations have gone into space and they all come back, amazingly enough, saying the very same thing: the earth is a small, blue place of profound beauty that we must take care of. For each, the journey into space, whatever its original intents and purposes, became above all a spiritual one." (after Al Reinhert's *For All Mankind*)

    _____

    _____

    _____

    _____

    _____

7. "What is technophobia really about? It's not an unhealthy and unjustified fear of confusing machinery that may break, bringing potential embarrassment or worse. No, it's a natural reaction to poorly designed machines." (after Donald Norman's *Defending Human Attributes in the Age of the Machine*)

    _____

    _____

    _____

    _____

    _____

8. "One of the usual things about education in mathematics in the United States is its relatively impoverished vocabulary. Whereas the student completing elementary school will already have a vocabulary for most disciplines of many hundreds, even thousands of words, the typical student will have a mathematics vocabulary of only a couple of dozen words." (after Marvin Minsky's *The Society of Mind*)

    _____

    _____

    _____

    _____

    _____

9. "Underlying all great works of art is the artist's completely private and unfathomable tenacity—his or her unrelenting pursuit of an idea, a feeling, or a vision beyond the boundaries where most of us would stop. Travelling into places beyond our ken, they return with artifacts that we can inspect in the safety of a gallery or museum. But just as we don't mistake a trip to the natural history museum for a visit to the jungle itself, nor should we mistake a visit to an art museum for the creative ferment of the artist's studio. The gilt-framed museum painting, hung in front of speechless crowds shuffling respectfully past, is no more alive than the stuffed museum lion, posed with its false glass eyes mocking menace and forever unmoving. And if we turn to ask the artists themselves about these pieces? They are nowhere to be seen, for they are packed and already gone." (after Thomas Murphy's essay, "Private Experience and Public Display" in *The Collected Works of T. D. Murphy*)

_____

_____

_____

_____

_____

10. "In archetypal symbolism, clothing represents *persona*, the first view the public gains of us. Persona is a kind of camouflage which lets others know only what we wish them to know about us, and nothing more. But the persona is not just a mask to hide behind, it is also a presence which eclipses the mundane personality. In this sense, persona or mask is an outward signal of rank, virtue, character, and authority." (after Clarissa Pinkola Estés's *Women Who Run with the Wolves*)

_____

_____

_____

_____

_____

MLA

Integrating Borrowed Material   **Refer to the Handbook chapter IX, pp. 267–271.**

Quotations are generally used to support and develop an idea already presented in your paper. For this exercise, first read the quotation provided and then develop a claim that can be supported and developed by the quotation. Second, briefly state your claim; and third, write a paragraph that employs all, or some, of the quotation provided to support and develop your claim.

Be sure to use a clear signal phrase (for example, using author name, authority, and selecting a precise and appropriate introductory verb such as "supports," "explains," "argues," etc.). Such signal phrases (1) help integrate the quotation smoothly into your own line of argument, (2) help your reader understand for what purpose the quotation is being used, and (3) help your reader distinguish your own thoughts from those of your quoted source.

For example:

Quotation and source: "The size of the 'hole' in the ozone layer would amaze most citizens." Peter Cannis, Director, Center for Atmospheric Study, in *The 1998 Annual Review of the Environment*, p. 47.

Claim:

> The ozone problem is serious and merits our attention.

Paragraph incorporating quotation:

> The steady diminishing of the ozone layer has caused the appearance of a vast area of thinning most often referred to as a "hole." Many scientists are concerned that the general population is not concerned and informed about the problem. Dr Peter Cannis, Director of the Center for Atmospheric Study, warned, "The size of the hole in the ozone layer would amaze most citizens" (47). It is, in fact, the size of North America.

1. Quotation and source: "The Information Superhighway will provide a general intellectual mobility for the American people that our national system of interstate highways has heretofore provided for transportation." Iam C. Piu, Founder, Americans for the 21st Century. Address to the National Press Club, Jan. 12, 2001: "The Next Twenty Years in U.S. Information Technology."

Claim:

_____

_____

Paragraph incorporating quotation:

_____

_____

_____

_____

_____

_____

_____

_____

_____

2. Quotation and source: "Though to our eyes in the early twenty-first century Henry David Thoreau lived in an America that seems wild, unspoiled, and largely undeveloped, to Thoreau this same world was one already in physical and moral decline, seemingly being devoured before his very eyes." Benjamin Austin, in *Perspective in American Life and Literature*, p. 38.

Claim:

_____

_____

Paragraph incorporating quotation:

_____

_____

_____

_____

_____

_____

_____

_____

_____

_____

3. Quotation and source: "It doesn't matter where you live. Long distances used to be a moat that both insulated and isolated people from workers on the other side of the world. But every day, technology narrows that moat inch by inch. Every person in the world is on the verge of becoming both a coworker and a competitor to every one of us. ... Technological change is going to reach out and sooner or later change something fundamental in your ... world." Andrew S. Grove, President and CEO, Intel Corporation, in *Only the Paranoid Survive*, 1997, p. 5.

Claim:

_____

_____

Paragraph incorporating quotation:

_____

_____

_____

_____

_____

_____

_____

_____

_____

MLA

1a, MLA In-Text Citations   Refer to the Handbook, pp. 303–308.

For each of the following exercises, write a passage incorporating the quoted material and giving an MLA-style in-text citation. Use signal phrases as indicated.

For example:

Format: Quote the following author using a signal phrase.

Author: Giuliano Procacci

Quote: "Yet it was not until 1930 that, for the first time in the history of Italy, the value of industrial production overtook that of agriculture."

Source: *History of the Italian People,* p. 379

Context: This is the only document by this author that is being used in the paper.

Possible Answer:

Of the gradual industrialization of Italy, Procacci notes that "it was not until 1930 that, for the first time in the history of Italy, the value of industrial production overtook that of agriculture" (379).

1. Format: Quote the following author **without** using a signal phrase.

   Author: Richard Adams

   Quote: "Human beings say, 'It never rains but it pours.' This is not very apt, for it frequently does rain without pouring. The rabbits' proverb is better expressed. They say, 'One cloud feels lonely.'"

   Source: *Watership Down,* fiction, chapter 23, p. 184

   Context: This is the only document by this author that is being used in the paper.

   _____

   _____

   _____

   _____

   _____

2. Format: Quote the following author using a signal phrase.

   Author: Richard Adams

   Quote: "Human beings say, 'It never rains but it pours.' This is not very apt, for it frequently does rain without pouring. The rabbits' proverb is better expressed. They say, 'One cloud feels lonely.'"

   Source: *Watership Down,* fiction, chapter 23, p. 184

   Context: This is one of two documents by this author that is being used in the paper.

   _____

   _____

   _____

   _____

   _____

3. Format: Quote the following authors **without** using a signal phrase.

   Authors: Charles Heimler and Charles Neal

   Quote: "A cloud is a collection of water droplets or ice crystals in the air. It is formed when water vapor is cooled and changed into water droplets or ice crystals."

   Source: *Principles of Science,* p. 234

   Context: This is the only document by these authors that is being used in this paper.

_____

_____

_____

_____

_____

4. Format: Quote the following authors using a signal phrase.

   Author(s):   Charles Heimler and Charles Neal

   Quote: "A cloud is a collection of water droplets or ice crystals in the air. It is formed when water vapor is cooled and changed into water droplets or ice crystals."

   Source: *Principles of Science,* p. 234

   Context: This is one of three documents by these authors that is being used in this paper.

_____

_____

_____

_____

_____

5. Format: Quote the following author using a signal phrase.

    Author: Reginald J. Symington

    Quote: "NATO's muddled expansion is so fraught with competing strategies that it has simultaneously threatened Moscow and made overtures to Russia to join the alliance itself."

    Source: "NATO at the Crossroads," in *Foreign Affairs,* April 1996, p. 267

    Context: This is one of two articles by this author that is being used in the paper.

_____

_____

_____

_____

_____

6. Format: Quote the following author using a signal phrase.

    Author: Allen Ginsberg

    Quote: "I saw the best minds of my generation destroyed by madness / starving hysterical naked."

    Source: "HOWL Parts I and Part II," poem, lines 1-2

    Context: This is the only piece by this author that is being used in the paper.

_____

_____

_____

_____

_____

7. Format: Quote the following author using a signal phrase.

   Author: Anne Tierney

   Quote: "Computers have only very recently become common outside narrowly defined locations such as academia, business, and the military. We are just beginning to understand what the age of 'personal computing' will mean to our culture."

   Source: Personal Interview, 22 July 2001

   Context: This is the only document by this author that is being used in the paper.

   _____

   _____

   _____

   _____

   _____

8. Format: Quote the following authors **without** using a signal phrase.

   Authors: Elizabeth McMahan, Susan Day, and Robert Funk

   Quote: "Rhythm can affect us powerfully. We respond almost automatically to the beat of a drum, the thumping of our heart, the pulsing of an engine. Poetic rhythm, usually more subtle, is made by repeating stresses and pauses."

   Source: *Literature and the Writing Process,* pp. 411–12

   Context: This is the only document by these authors that is being used in this paper.

   _____

   _____

   _____

   _____

   _____

9. Format: Quote the following authors using a signal phrase.

   Authors: Elizabeth McMahan, Susan Day, and Robert Funk

   Quote: "Rhythm can affect us powerfully. We respond almost automatically to the beat of a drum, the thumping of our heart, the pulsing of an engine. Poetic rhythm, usually more subtle, is made by repeating stresses and pauses."

   Source: *Literature and the Writing Process,* pp. 411–12

   Context: This is one of three documents by these authors that is being used in this paper.

   _____

   _____

   _____

   _____

   _____

10. Format: Quote the following author using a signal phrase.

   Authors: Corporate Author, Solar United Now (SUN)

   Quote: "Solar power is rapidly becoming financially viable primarily due to increasing solar conversion efficiencies and improved manufacturing. It would in fact compete favorably now with coal and oil if it were not for those industries' 'subsidies' in the form of federal policies, laws, and tax code provisions."

   Source: *A Solar Primer,* p. 44

   Context: This is the only document by this author that is being used in the paper.

   _____

   _____

   _____

   _____

   _____

MLA

2, MLA Manuscript Format   **Refer to the Handbook, pp. 325–336.**

A page of a student paper that should follow MLA guidelines appears on the next page. Lettered line segments mark a number of elements on the page. Complete the following list by indicating next to each letter the appropriate margin, position, or spacing. The first one is done for you as an example.

There are eleven additional formatting flaws in this sample page. List them and describe what should have been done instead. Use the spaces provided.

    (a) <u>top of page</u> to <u>last name/page number</u>: 1/2 inch

1.   **(b)**   top and bottom margins:

2.   **(c)**   line spacing:

3.   **(d)**   left margin:

4.   **(e)**   right margin:

5.   **(f)** _____

6.   **(g)** _____

7.   **(h)** _____

8.   **(i)** _____

9.   **(j)** _____

10.   **(k)** _____

11.   **(l)** _____

(b)

Lorem ipsum dolor sit amet, consectetuer adipiscing

(c) **(g)** Elit, sed diam nonummy nibh euismod tincidunt ut laoreet

Dolore magna aliquam erat volutpat.

(h) MAJOR HEADING

Duis autem vel eum irirure dolor in hendrerit in vulpputate

velit esse molestie consequat, abitando quest'anno in

toscano. Vel ilium doloreeu feugiat nulla facilisis at

vero eros et accumsan – iusto odio dignissim qui   **(e)**

blandit.

(d)(j)

(i) Subheading

Ut wisi enim ad minim veniam, quis nostrud exerci tation

ullamcorper suscipit lobortis nisl ut aliquip ex ea

commodo consequat, Duis autem vel eum iriure dolor in

hendrerit in vulputate velit esse moletie; consequat,

vel illum dolore eu feugiat nulla facilisis at veto eros

et accumsan et iusto odio dignissim qui blandit praesent

luptatum:

> **(k)** "Delenit augue duis dolore te feugait nulla
> facilisi. Lorem ipsum dolor sit amet,
> consdectetuer adipscing elit, sed...nonummy
> aliquam erat volutpat. Ut wisi eniom ad minim
> veniam, quis nostrud aliquip ex ea commodo
> consequat." **(l)**

Duis autem vel eum iriure dolor in hendrerit in vulputate

velit esse molestie consequat, vel illum dolore eu

(b)

MLA

1c MLA Works Cited   Refer to the Handbook, pp. 309–325.

Using the following sources, create a works cited page in MLA format.

1. **Article Title:** Hamlet, reconciliation, and the just state (Critical essay)
   Author: Grace Tiffany
   Journal: Renascence: Essays on Values in Literature. Vol 58, issue #2, in winter 2005. begins on p. 111 and continues for 23 pages
   Found in: Expanded Academic Index in Info Trac database on February 26, 2007

2. **Article Title:** Prince of self-pity. (Hamlet) (Critical Essay)
   Author: Allan Massie
   Journal: Spectator, July 15, 2006. No pages given
   Found in: Expanded Academic Index in Info Trac database on February 26, 2007

3. **Article Title:** Shakespeare's Hamlet (Critical Essay)
   Author: Mark Taylor
   Journal: The Explicator fall 2006, vol 65, issue #1. Begins on p. 4 and continues for 4 pages
   Found in: Expanded Academic Index in Info Trac database on February 26, 2007

4. **Book Title:** Hamlet: Complete, authoritative texts with biographical and historical contexts, critical history, and essays from five contemporary critical perspectives/William Shakespeare
   Edited by: Susanne L. Wofford
   Publisher: Bedford Books of St. Martin's Press in Boston
   Copyright: 1994

5. **Book Title:** Shakespeare 400: essays by American scholars on the anniversary of the poet's birth
   Author: James Gilmer McManaway
   Publisher: Holt, Rinehart, and Winston in New York
   Copyright: 1964

6. Hamlet Found on website Literature Network, William Shakespeare http://www.online-literature.com/shakespeare/hamlet on February 26, 2007

7. Hamlet Found on website http://www.shakespeare-literature.com/Hamlet/index.html on February 26, 2007

CHAPTER XII   APA–STYLE DOCUMENTATION
AND FORMAT

APA

Questions   **Refer to the Handbook, chapter XII.**

Respond to the following short answer questions.

1. What do the letters in the abbreviation APA stand for?

2. What is the two-part system of documentation for APA?

3. Why are in-text citations used in APA-style documentation?

4. In most APA in-text citations, what two elements of the source are included?

5. If you are citing a source with more than one author, how do you present the in-text citation?

6. If you are citing an electronic source, how do you present the in-text citation?

7. What is the list of sources in an APA-style paper titled?

8. In what order are citations given in the list of sources in an APA-style paper?

9. What are the formatting features of the list of sources in an APA-style paper?

10. Describe the manuscript format for an APA-style paper.

APA

2, APA Manuscript Format

Refer to the Handbook, pp. 351–360.

A page of a student paper that should follow APA guidelines appears on the next page. Lettered line segments mark a number of elements on the page. Complete the following list by indicating next to each letter the appropriate margin, position, or spacing. The first one is done for you as an example.

In addition, there are eleven formatting flaws in this sample page. List them and describe what should have been done instead. Use the spaces provided.

    (a) <u>top of page</u> to <u>last name/page number:</u> 1/2inch

1. **(b)** top and bottom margins:

2. **(c)** line spacing:

3. **(d)** left margin:

4. **(e)** right margin:

5. **(f)** _____

6. **(g)** _____

7. **(h)** _____

8. **(i)** _____

9. **(j)** _____

10. **(k)** _____

11. **(l)** _____

(a)

(f)

(b)

Smith page 3

Lorem ipsum dolor sit amet, Consectetuer adipiscing elit, sed

(c)

diam nonummy Nibh euismod tincidunt ut laoreet dolore magna

aliquam erat volutpat.

MAJOR HEADING **(k)**

(h) Duis autem vel eum irirure dolor in hendrerit in vulpputate velit esse molestie consequat, abitando quest'anno in toscano. Vel ilium doloreeu feugiat nulla facilisis at vero eros et accumsan – iusto odio dignissim qui blandit.

(e)

(d)

Subheading (l)

Ut wisi enim ad minim veniam, quis nostrud exerci tation ullamcorper suscipit lobortis nisl ut aliquip ex ea commodo consequat, Duis autem vel eum iriure dolor in hendrerit in vulputate velit esse moletie; consequat, vel illum dolore eu feugiat nulla facilisis at veto eros et accumsan et iusto odio dignissim qui blandit praesent luptatum:

> **(i)** "Delenit augue duis dolore te feugait nulla facilisi. Lorem ipsum dolor sit amet, consdectetuer adipscing elit, sed...nonummy aliquam erat volutpat. Ut wisi eniom ad minim veniam, quis nostrud aliquip ex ea commodo consequat." **(j)**

(g)

Duis autem vel eum iriure dolor in hendrerit in vulputate velit esse molestie consequat, vel illum dolore Vel illum dolore eu feugiat nulla facilisis at veto eros et accumsar, et iusto odio dignissim qui blandit.

(b)

APA

Reference Page

Refer to the Handbook, pp. 341-351.

Using the following sources, create a reference page in APA format.

1. **Author**: Deborah Brandt
   Title: Literacy in American Lives
   Place of Publication: New York
   Publisher: Cambridge University Press
   Date of publication: 2001
   Number of pages: 258 pages

2. **Author:** Samuel Greengard
   Article Title: Getting Rid of the Paper Chase
   Title: Workforce
   Date of Publication: Nov. 1999 Vol. 3 Issue 12
   Page number: 69
   Retrieved from: Baker College General Business File ASAP
   Date retrieved: Feb. 24, 2002
   Web address:
   www.web3.onfotrc.g.../purl=rcl_GBFM_0_A57815216&dyn=27!arfmt?sw_aep=falcon_
   baker

3. **Authors:** Abigail J. Sellen and Richard H.R. Harper
   Title: The Myth of the Paperless Office
   Place of Publication: Cambridge, Massachusetts
   Publisher: The MIT Press
   Date of Publication: 2002

4. **Author**: Trish Glazebrook
   Title: From…to Nature, Artifacts to Technology: Heidegger on Aristotle, Galileo, and Newton.
   Journal Title: The Southern Journal of Philosophy
   Date of Publication: 2000 no volume or page numbers given

5. **Author**: Unknown
   Title: Our Evolving Culture: A Short History of Four Simple Ideas and How They Changed the Way We Dream, Travel, Learn, and Walk
   Title of Magazine: Time
   Date of Publication: Dec. 31, 1999
   Pages: 173+

6. **Author**: Unknown
    Title: Surprising Many, Paper Use Soars with Internet Growth
    Date: April 22, 1999
    Web address: www.papercom.org/press6.htm>.

7. **Author**: Anne E. Platt
    Title: Waste Threatens the World's Seas
    Title of Magazine: World Watch
    Date of Publication: Jan. /Feb. 1995
    Reprinted in: Garbage and Waste: Current Controversies
    Editor: Charles Cozic
    Place of Publication: San Diego
    Publisher: Greenhaven Press
    Date of Publication: 1997
    Pages: 36-44

CHAPTER XIII CMS DOCUMENTATION AND FORMAT CSE DOCUMENTATION

CMS

Questions Refer to the Handbook, pp. 361–382.

Respond to the following short answer questions.

1. What do the letters in the abbreviation CMS stand for?

2. What is the two-part system of documentation for CMS?

3. Why are endnotes used in CMS documentation?

4. The first time a source is cited in CMS, what elements of the source are included?

5. If you are citing a source with more than one author, how do you present the endnote?

6. If you are citing an electronic source, how do you present the endnote?

7. What is the list of sources in a CMS paper titled?

8. In what order are citations given in the list of sources in a CMS paper?

9. What are the formatting features of the list of sources in a CMS paper?

10. Describe the manuscript format for a CMS paper.

CMS

Bibliography   **Refer to the Handbook, pp. 362–371.**

Using the following sources, create a bibliography page in CMS format..

1. **Editor:** David L. Poremba
    Title: If I Am Found Dead: Michigan Voices from the Civil War
    Place of Publication: Ann Arbor, MI
    Publisher: Ann Arbor Media Group
    Date of Publication: 2006

2. **Author:** Kenneth P. Williams
    Title: Lincoln Finds a General: A Military Study of the Civil War
    Place of Publication: Bloomington, IN
    Publisher: Indiana University Press
    Date of Publication: 1949

3. **Author:** John Maynard Smith
    Article Title: The Origin of Altruism
    Title: Nature
    Date of Publication: 1998 volume 393 issue none
    Page numbers: 639-640

4. **Authors:** Mark A. Hlatky, Derek Boothroyd, Eric Vittinghoff, Penny Sharp, and Mary A. Whooley
    Article Title: Quality-of-Life and Depressive Symptoms
    Title: Journal of the American Medical Association
    Date of Publication: February 6, 2002 volume 287 no. 5
    Date Retrieved: Accessed January 7, 2007
    Web address: http://jama.ama-assn.org/issues/v287n5/rfull/joc10108.html

5. **Author:** William S. Niederkorn
    Article Title: A scholar recants on his "Shakespeare" discovery
    Title: New York Times
    Date of Publication: June 20, 2002
    Page numbers: not given; Arts section, Midwest edition

6. **Author:** Tyler Anbinder
    Article Title: Which Poor Man's Fight? Immigrants and the
    Federal Conscription of 1863
    Title: Civil War History
    Date of Publication: December 2006 volume 52 issue 4
    Page numbers: 344 (29)
    Database: Expanded Academic Index in InfoTrac database
    Retrieved Date: March 15, 2007
    Web Address: http://80-find.galegroup.com.ezproxy.falcon.edu/itx/basicSearch

CSE

Questions Refer to the Handbook, pp. 382–392.

Respond to the following short answer questions.

1. What do the letters in the abbreviation CSE stand for?

2. What is the two-part system of documentation for CSE?

3. What are the three different systems for referring to a reference within a paper in CSE-style documentation?

4. If you are citing a source with more than one author, how do you present the in-text citation using the name-year system?

5. What is the list of sources in a CSE-style paper titled?

6. If you use the citation-sequence system for your in-text citations, in what order are citations given in the list of sources in a CSE-style paper?

7. If you use the name-year system for your in-text citations, in what order are citations given in the list of sources in a CSE-style paper?

8. If you use the citation-name system for your in-text citations, in what order are citations given in the list of sources in a CSE-style paper?

9. What are the formatting features of the list of sources in a CSE-style paper?

10. If you use the CSE citation-name system, describe the process for preparing both in-text and list of sources citations.

CSE

References page   **Refer to the Handbook, pp. 384–392.**

Using the following sources, create a references page in CSE format.

1. **Author:** T. E. Philippi, P.M. Dixon, and B. E. Taylor
   Article Title: Detecting Trends in Species Composition
   Title: Ecological Applications
   Date of Publication: May 1998 volume 8 issue 2
   Page numbers: 300-8
   Retrieved Date: March 15, 2007
   Web Address: http://www.esajournals.org/esaonline

2. **Author:** C. Hilton-Taylor, Compiler
   Title: 2000 IUCN Red List of Threatened Species
   Date of Publication: 2000
   Retrieved Date: April 2, 2007
   Web Address: http://www.redlist.org

3. **Author:** L. D. Mech
   Title: The Arctic Wolf: Living with the Pack
   Place of Publication: Stillwater, MN
   Publisher: Voyageur Press
   Date of Publication: 1998
   Number of Pages: 128

4. **Editors:** M. L. Reaka-Kudla, D. E. Wilson, and E. O. Wilson
   Title: Biodiversity II: Understanding and Protecting Our Biological Resources
   Place of Publication: Washington, D.C.
   Publisher: Joseph Henry Press
   Date of Publication: 1997
   Number of Pages: 551

5. **Author:** C.K. Yoon
   Article Title: DNA Clues Improve Outlook for Red Wolf
   Title: New York Times
   Date of Publication: December 26, 2000
   Pages: Section F: 10 (col 1)

6. **Authors:** J. Cox and R. T. Engstrom
   Article Title: Influence of the Spatial Pattern of Conserved Lands on the Persistence of a Large Population of Red-Cockaded Woodpeckers
   Title: Biological Conservation
   Date of Publication: 2001 volume 100 issue 1
   Pages: 137-150

XIV ESL BASICS

AN IMPORTANT REMINDER FOR STUDENTS: Because of the flexibility of the English language, there may be more than one way to correct the errors in each exercise. This is particularly true in this chapter. If you have any questions about your answers versus the ones supplied in the Selected Answers section, please ask your instructor. Very likely there will be other students with the same or similar questions.

ESL

1a, Modals

Refer to the Handbook, pp. 393–394.

Correct the use of modal auxiliaries in the following sentences.

For example: Nick will not to swim in the lake with us.

Correction: **Nick will not swim in the lake with us.**

1.   In one hour I be done.

2.   You will to see me there tonight.

3.   I should can finish this novel before class.

4.   We cannot to come to the party.

5.   When I was growing up, my family will usually take a trip in the summer.

6.   Elly is knowing how to operate the slide projector.

7.   In ten minutes the eggs be ready.

8.   Rizal can sings very well.

9.   I can have to leave early.

10.   He must cleaning up before he can go.

ESL

1b, Perfect Tenses

Refer to the Handbook, pp. 394–395.

Correct the use of perfect tenses in the following sentences.

For example: She have found a nice new apartment.

Correction: She has found a nice new apartment.

1.   They have travel too much this year to want to go on another trip soon.

2.   We has expecting you yesterday.

3.   Bill goes to the movies frequently; he will have saw the latest comedy already.

4.   Chloë had sang in the choir for three years before she was chosen to be its director.

5.   Suzanne have brung me flowers every year on my birthday.

6.   The newspapers has reported on the new president closely.

7.   As of next spring, our organization will had support the children's hospital for twenty-five years.

8.   I have drove on this road before.

9.   They has gave Paul an award two years in a row now.

10.   She have raised a child even while enrolled in school.

ESL

1c, Progressive Tenses   **Refer to the Handbook, pp. 395–397.**

Correct the use of progressive tenses in the following sentences.

For example: Lola been coming here every day.

Correction: Lola has been coming here every day.

1.   John seeing Reno for the first time.

2.   Sheila are giving her friends dancing lessons.

3.   The ozone layer been thinning because of the release of harmful chemicals.

4.   Han is being happy today.

5.   Sanga had be thinking calculus was easy until he took the midterm exam.

6.   Jason is gone to the new play tomorrow night.

7.   They will working on the scenery this afternoon.

8.   By the time Mr. Tottle retires next year, he will been teaching at NBHS for thirty-eight years.

9.   They be discussing Iris Dement's newest record album.

10.   Anita been cooking her favorite dinner all afternoon.

ESL

1d, Passive Voice 1   **Refer to the Handbook, pp. 397–398.**

Correct the use of the passive voice in the following sentences.

For example: The siren was heared by everyone on the street.

Correction: **The siren was heard by everyone on the street.**

1.   The NBA championship was winned by San Antonio this year.

2.   Africa is visit by many Americans.

3.   We were sitted by the hostess.

4.   Many books now is published only in paperback.

5.   Every student are expected to do well in his or her studies.

6.   Many issues is discuss by the president's cabinet.

7.   John were bedridden because of the flu.

8.   The national anthem was singed by Placido Domingo.

9.   My pants were burnt when I ironed with the temperature too high.

10.   The night course were added because many people couldn't attend during the day.

ESL

1d, Passive Voice 2   **Refer to the Handbook, pp. 397–398.**

Rewrite the following passive voice sentences in the active voice.

For example: The siren was heard by everyone on the street.

Correction: **Everyone on the street heard the siren.**

1.   My backpack was lost yesterday by Terusuke.

2.   The fountain is seen by many commuters every day.

3.   *Carmen* was written by Bizet.

4.   Reading is enjoyed by many people.

5.   Money was scrupulously saved by my parents.

6.   A good time was had by everyone.

7.   Affordable housing was spoken about by the Birmingham City Council at every meeting.

8.   The satellite was boosted into orbit by the shuttle *Endeavor*.

9.   The crowd was thrilled by Eminem's performance.

10.   *Walden* was written by Henry David Thoreau during the period 1845–54.

ESL

1e, Two-Word Verbs   **Refer to the Handbook, pp. 398–399.**

Correct the two-word verbs in the following sentences.

For example: Phil came a helpful article across.

Correction: Phil came across a helpful article.

1. Where's the newspaper? Oh, John threw away it.

2. The teacher called the student on.

3. Because of the extensive fire damage, the fire marshal ordered the building's owners to tear down it.

4. Simone heard her best friend from.

5. Why doesn't he pick someone on his own size?

6. The aspirin helped me get the cold over.

7. When you are in Santa Fe, don't forget to look up me.

8. Look my cat after while I am away.

9. The TV is too loud; please turn down it.

10. My dad learned that smoking was unhealthy, so he gave up it.

ESL

1f, Verbals **Refer to the Handbook, pp. 400-402.**

Correct the verbals in the following sentences.

For example: His father cautioned him using the crosswalk always.

Correction: His father cautioned him always to use the crosswalk.

    OR: His father cautioned him about always using the crosswalk.

1.   They agreed come over here before the game.

2.   Josef misses himself to eat home-cooked meals.

3.   The boss permitted to take time off when my sister was married.

4.   I imagine to fly is wonderful.

5.   When I finish to eat, I'll read to you.

6.   Please think about to save money for college.

7.   Eriq is beginning sounding good on the piano.

8.   Sam manages living well on a modest income.

9.   Otto's parents invited me come with them to the show.

10.   My best friend suggested to see the school's career counselors before going to the interview.

ESL

2a–c, Count and Noncount Nouns 1   **Refer to the Handbook, pp. 402–403.**

Correct the use of count and noncount nouns in the following sentences.

For example: John bought two beefs at the butcher.

Correction: John bought two pounds of beef at the butcher.

1.   Gordon knows many local history.

2.   How many breads did Orlo ask us to pick up?

3.   Howard used two hundred pails of sands to build his huge sand castle.

4.   Guadalupe said much machines are built there.

5.   Don't put too many salt in the soup!

6.   We received many, many snows here last winter.

7.   My car used only 7 gallons of gasolines for the 300-mile trip.

8.   An information can be stored in a computer.

9.   The United States mixes much cultures.

10.   My grandfather and I cooked fourteen pound of tomato.

ESL

2a–b, Count and Noncount Nouns 2   **Refer to the Handbook, pp. 402–403.**

Correct the use of count and noncount nouns in the following sentences.

For example: Sally didn't have enough quarter for the parking meter.

Correction: Sally didn't have enough quarters for the parking meter.

1.   Gianni lost his cashes through a hole in his pocket.

2.   Their new furnitures are beautiful.

3.   Are there much students in your history class?

4.   Is Karen still looking for the place to live?

5.   The poet read her poems with a lot of confidences.

6.   How many rain fell here last month?

7.   For this class there is a lot of book.

8.   She said she would be here in two minute.

9.   There is not much times before our mid-term exam.

10.   I read that everyone should drink six glass of water every day.

ESL

2c–d, Articles   **Refer to the Handbook, pp. 403–405.**

Correct the use of articles (definite, indefinite) in the following sentences. In some instances, the correction may involve deleting the article.

For example: I moved to United States to find the good job with a fair pay.

Correction: I moved to the United States to find a good job with fair pay.

1.   Hour ago he left for the office.

2.   A president is the former governor of Texas.

3.   When she finishes the high school, she wants to travel before finding an employment.

4.   It was an hot day so we went to a beach.

5.   She worked for the General Electric before joining an Intel.

6.   Please pick me up pound of the coffee when you're at the market.

7.   The Harry Connick, Jr., plays a piano and sings too.

8.   Vietnam War still seems very recent to me.

9.   The Honorable Judge Hotalling presided at hearing.

10.   Bring towel and swimming suit to the party.

ESL

2d, Definite Article   **Refer to the Handbook, pp. 404–405.**

Correct the use of the definite article in the following sentences.

For example: I moved to the Chicago when I was seven years old.

Correction: I moved to Chicago when I was seven years old.

1.   Please pass some ketchup.

2.   Mount Katahdin is highest peak in Maine.

3.   I saw professor who won Nobel Prize last year.

4.   The hockey is very popular here.

5.   I saw the Bob walking down the hall just a minute ago.

6.   I arrive at the work by 8 a.m. every day.

7.   After graduating, Francine was hired by the NASA.

8.   Dora did not sing loudly, but her voice was best in the chorus.

9.   I read last week that the calcium is important in a diet.

10.   Montana is "A Big Sky State."

ESL

3a, Cumulative Adjectives

Refer to the Handbook, pp. 406.

Correct the word order of the adjectives in the following items.

For example: a brown big house

Correction: a big brown house

1.   a pearl white long necklace

2.   my new first bicycle

3.   square five small buildings

4.   a brick ancient fireplace

5.   triangular large seven windows

6.   a nineteenth-century elegant waltz

7.   a wooden white fence

8.   the German most knowledgeable scientist

9.   some small older cabs

10.   the hottest summer five days

ESL

3b, Present and Past Participles

Refer to the Handbook, pp. 406–407.

Correct the following sentences by changing past and present participles as necessary.

For example: The NBA finals always are excited.

Correction: **The NBA finals always are exciting.**

1.   Lola found the novel's ending surprised.

2.   The winter winds here are very dried.

3.   Sofia found organic chemistry fascinated.

4.   Jackie's remarks annoying me.

5.   The kitchen scene in *Jurassic Park* was frightened.

6.   Many visitors find the highways around Los Angeles confused.

7.   The ocean water refreshing me.

8.   Jean saw depressed similarities in the history of the 1930s and the 1990s.

9.   I found Pacino's performance engaged.

10.   Our hike into a strong wind all day left us exhausting.

ESL

3c, Adverbs   **Refer to the Handbook, pp. 407–408.**

Correct the placement of adverbs in the following sentences.

For example: The food there always is good.

Correction: **The food there is always good.**

1.   The president addresses traditionally the Congress in January.

2.   There seems never to be enough time.

3.   My older sister always is helpful.

4.   I drove enough fast to get to work on time.

5.   Ving went typically to the museum with his father.

6.   Peter gave happily his present to his mother.

7.   After the rain shower, my clothes were enough wet to be wrung.

8.   My dentist fails never to remind me to floss as well as brush.

9.   John mailed early his package.

10.   When she drove, she was focused extremely.

ESL

4a–c, Prepositions 1   **Refer to the Handbook, pp. 408–409.**

Correct the use of prepositions in the following sentences. The correction may include removing prepositions as well as adding them.

For example: I prefer to travel in train rather than in plane.

Correction: I prefer to travel by train rather than by plane.

1.   I went the movies nearly every week last summer.

2.   Francesca reads on the newspaper to improve her English.

3.   When we first moved at Toronto, I missed Hong Kong very much.

4.   Sari shops the grocery store every day.

5.   After his trip in Somalia, the landscape in New England looked at very green to him.

6.   Doug told me he works on his uncle's store.

7.   Though I had read Shakespeare in translation before coming to the States, I am finding it entirely new for English.

8.   The downtown bus stops at here at quarter past and quarter of the hour.

9.   Sergei finished his story by time for class.

10.   I would like to go the museum this Friday.

ESL

4d–f, Prepositions 2   **Refer to the Handbook, pp. 409–410.**

Correct the use of prepositions in the following sentences. The correction may include removing prepositions as well as adding them.

For example: We called off our picnic because rain.

Correction: We called off our picnic because of rain.

1.   Frederico was aware on the problem.

2.   My brother's new glasses are for to read.

3.   I walked as far Main Street before discovering that I had left my wallet at home.

4.   How much is that equal of in dollars?

5.   I like to paint as to well draw.

6.   Due fog, the airport was closed.

7.   "Come along me," called Gisela to Dave.

8.   Omar was very proud for his diploma.

9.   Addition to this book, you'll need that one.

10.   Paul said, "After to exercise, stretch out and then shower."

ESL

5a–b, Omitted Verbs and Subjects

Refer to the Handbook, pp. 410–411.

Correct the following sentences by ensuring that each clause has one subject and that linking verbs are present when needed.

For example: My house, which was built in 1922, it has many architectural details not found in newer houses.

Correction: My house, which was built in 1922, has many architectural details not found in newer houses.

1. My school has three libraries. Will begin construction of a fourth soon.

2. Dirk's whole family very amusing.

3. The baseball league, it begins its season next week.

4. This reading assignment very long.

5. The crickets in the trees in my neighborhood they sing all day.

6. If clichés not true, why are they so often repeated?

7. Great-Uncle Tom, who loved to invent things, he was always fun to visit.

8. Dan's notebook, containing all his laboratory notes, it has been missing since yesterday.

9. My dinner, left too long in the oven, it became a black brick, unrecognizable as food.

10. Our team won both games last week. Won last weekend, too.

ESL

5c, Expletives   **Refer to the Handbook, pp. 411–412.**

Correct the use of expletives and verb agreement in the following sentences.

For example: Is a beautiful day today.

Correction: **It is a beautiful day today.**

1.   There is three interstate highways into downtown Atlanta.

2.   Here is my top choices for the position.

3.   Here are the best recipe I have for turkey stuffing.

4.   Is unlikely to rain when the sky is so clear.

5.   There have many golf courses in Chittenden County.

6.   Though the park is crowded, is still fun to be here.

7.   She said there was two puppies for sale.

8.   There is three stores on my block.

9.   There are much speculation about why the dinosaurs disappeared.

10.   Is true he won't run for another term as mayor?

ESL

6b, Questions with *Who*, *Whom*, and *What*   **Refer to the Handbook, pp. 413.**

Correct the word order and helping verbs in the following questions containing *who*, *whom*, and *what*.

For example: What birds to migrate cause?

Correction: What causes birds to migrate?

1.   Who are coming to dinner?

2.   Whom created the congressional gridlock?

3.   Whom the president nominated?

4.   Who today's mail brings in?

5.   What the committee do?

6.   Who is believing that explanation?

7.   To who they sent the package?

8.   What tides and currents in the ocean create?

9.   Who take the bus to school?

10.   What Murray listens to on the radio?

ESL

6c, Indirect Questions 1   **Refer to the Handbook, pp. 413–414.**

For each sentence, find the indirect question and rewrite it as a direct question.

For example: I don't know what time she's planning to arrive.

Answer: What time is she planning to arrive?

1.   The proposal is unclear about how they will finance the new daycare center.

2.   He thought he knew which astronomer first identified black holes.

3.   My grandmother explained why my family came to this country in 1848.

4.   She saw where the smoke was coming from.

5.   Gena wonders how the U.S. Congress differs from the British Parliament.

6.   I wasn't sure when Cassius Clay changed his name to Muhammad Ali.

7.   The engineers investigated how gravity affected the growth of crystals.

8.   Robert didn't know when we could visit the Dow Planetarium in Montreal.

9.   I would like to know what makes a good bus driver.

10.   Paola asked me what I would give her for her birthday.

ESL

6c, Indirect Questions 2   **Refer to the Handbook, pp. 413–414.**

Correct the following indirect questions by using proper word order and verbs.

For example: The lead story traced how has drug use changed in the last decade.

Correction: The lead story traced how drug use has changed in the last decade.

1.   He asked me are you coming or not.

2.   Rupert wasn't sure when did the Battle of Hastings occur.

3.   We tried to see where did the rocket go.

4.   The committee researched why has the cost of education outpaced inflation in the last ten years.

5.   Everice asked do you enjoy playing racquetball.

6.   The reporter asked when will we see the mayor's new budget.

7.   I don't understand how does this lock work.

8.   My nephew wondered did I want to go to the park with him.

9.   Tamara is not sure will you like pistachio ice cream.

10.   I asked myself how can he be so late?

ESL

6d, Reported Speech   **Refer to the Handbook, pp. 414–416.**

For the following sentences, rewrite the direct quotations as reported speech and the reported speech as direct quotation.

Reported: He said he'd been looking forward to meeting my family for a long time.

Direct: He said, "I've been looking forward to meeting your family for a long time."

Direct: "Where were you last night," asked Joseph, "when I needed a ride home?"

Reported: Joseph asked where I was last night when he needed a ride home.

1.   "I love zucchini," said Nino, "almost as much as I love peppers."

2.   Bob told me that he was working in the library five nights per week.

3.   "Roger has played a faltering but passionate cello for years," Erin stated with a grin.

4.   Mary announced that she would be running in the New York Marathon this year.

5.   "Wait for the third quarter results," said the company spokesperson.

6.   Annika observed that she had not seen many men in bikinis in beer commercials.

7.   "Will the economy improve this year, Mr. Bernanke?" the anxious Senate Finance Committee member asked.

8.   The reporter asked the candidate whether or not she would vote for House Resolution 143.

9.   "I may not have the money to travel home for Thanksgiving this year," Willy told me.

10.   Whenever my grandmother found me working late, she would tell me that two hours at night were worth one hour in the morning.

ESL

6e, Conditional Sentences   Refer to the Handbook, pp. 416–418.

Correct the verbs in the following conditional sentences.

For example: When air warms, it will rise.

Correction: When air warms, it rises.

1.   If he sees a shooting star, he will make a wish.

2.   If you practice enough, you could join a band.

3.   If I had practiced more, I may have my own band.

4.   Wherever Fleetwood Mac performed last year, they find big audiences.

5.   If Al Gore had been elected, what changes would he make?

6.   If you were the laboratory's teaching assistant, what will you do?

7.   Whenever she has trouble sleeping, she will drink some warm milk and go right back to bed.

8.   If we get lost on the way to the airport, we would miss our plane.

9.   When I exercise at least three days per week, my back will never bother me.

10.   Unless I hear from him today, I am assuming he is coming tomorrow.

XV GLOSSARY

Glossary

Usage 1   Refer to the Handbook, pp. 419–428.

Correct the errors in word usage in the following sentences.

Example: The Pulitzer Prize is a honor.

Answer: The Pulitzer Prize is an honor.

1. I thought we could leave, but Joe ain't ready to go.

2. The reason Nicholas loved music of all types is because he was in a music appreciation class.

3. Although I set out twenty tomato plants this summer, I should of planted at least thirty.

4. Being that the show on Channel 42 at 10 tonight is very interesting, he will be sure to set his TIVO to record it.

5. Jason can't hardly get his work done because of school.

6. I like all winter sports accept skiing, which is too challenging for me.

7. The traffic was so light that we had no problem getting their on time.

8. No one responded, so I have no idea whose coming.

9. The ozone layer has decreased alot in the past twenty years.

10. Each year the ocean currents cut further into the beach.

11. How will I be effected by the changes in the curriculum?

12. Students can choose between math, science, and history for their elective.

13. Little children want to do things by theirselves.

14. Hopefully, I will pass this class.

15. She was suppose to stay with the group, but she wandered away from it.

GLOSSARY

Usage 2   **Refer to the Handbook, pp. 419–428.**

Replace the italicized word—used incorrectly—in each of the following sentences with the correct word. Then identify the part of speech and write a short definition for both the incorrect and correct words. Consult a dictionary if necessary.

Example: Albert Einstein was an *imminent* scholar.

Answer: Albert Einstein was an eminent scholar.

imminent (adj): existing within or inherent

eminent (adj): outstanding

imminant (adj): about to happen

1.   What are the *affects* of the new spending bill?

2.   Even if you disagree strongly with him, please be *civic*.

3.   Emile *can't hardly* read without going to sleep.

4.   *Irregardless* of her efforts, Jane still didn't get a raise.

5.   Paul, carried away by the emotional appeal of his own argument, went off on a *tangible*.

6.   Despite the effort to keep the peace talks going, the ambassador will *loose* the agreement between the two countries.

7.   This apartment is cold because its walls have no *isolation*.

8.   My new car uses almost 50 percent less fuel than my old one; its engine is much more *proficient*.

9.   The facilitator successfully *meditated* the dispute.

10.   George is *libel* to come in here at any moment.

SELECTED ANSWERS TO EXERCISES

I. THE WRITING PROCESS

WRIT PROC 4c Proofreading

See your instructor.

WRIT PROC 1d, 1f, and 2c

See your instructor.

II. WRITING IN COLLEGE AND BEYOND

ARGUE 4, Distinguishing between Fact and Opinion (F=Fact; O=Opinion)

1. The World Trade Center tragedy affected the United States more than other countries. (F)

2. The terrorist attack on the World Trade Center could have been prevented. (O)

3. Country music is the best style of music for dancing. (O)

4. Studying history is not relevant to today's workplace. (O)

5. The legal drinking age in most states is twenty-one. (F)

ARGUE 4a, Facts versus Claims

These are possible answers for claims.

1. (claim) Euthanasia is a right that every American should have the option of electing.

2. (fact) Some animal rights advocates object to the use of animals for medical research and testing.

   (claim) It is immoral to use animals for medical research and testing.

3. (fact) The use of grades is traditional in American schools.

   (claim) The use of grades stifles creativity in American schools.

4. (fact) Snowboarding became an Olympic medal sport in 1998.

   (claim) The designation of snowboarding in 1998 as an Olympic sport will serve to promote this sport's development.

5. (fact) U.S. immigration policy has changed since September 11, 2001.

(claim) To the detriment of our nation, US. immigration policy has changed since September 11, 2001.

ARGUE 4b, Logical Appeals

1. Every time I go to the hockey game, I come down with a cold; therefore, hockey games cause colds. (Post Hoc, Ergo Propter Hoc)

2. If everyone would be a vegetarian, no one would have health problems. (Oversimplification)

3. College is hard because there is a lot of hard work. (Begging the Question)

4. The governments of Russia and China are similar because they are near each other. (False Analogy)

5. Everyone should try the South Beach Diet because that is what all the supermodels use. (Band Wagon)

ONLINE WRITING 5a , E-mail

1. Subject line is blank; it should instead provide some useful indicator of the message's contents.

2. "Prof." instead of Professor—this is the first of a series of excessively informal choices made by the writer. Note that this is a message from a student to his professor; it should not be overly informal. The same standards generally apply to e-mail at work.

3. "w/" instead of "with"; this style is too informal.

4. "u" instead of "you"; this style is too informal

5. "b/c" instead of "because"; again, this style is too informal.

PUBLIC WRITING 7a, Formatting a Business Letter

1. top of page to top of return address: 6–12 line spaces (use this variation to balance the letter visually on the page from top to bottom)

2. line spacing: single-spaced throughout

Check spaces between blocks as they should not all be the same; that is, add space between the date and internal address; internal address and salutation; between the saluation and body text; between the last text block and the close; between the close and signature; and between the signature and notations (if any).

3. Keep paragraphing format style consistent (blocked)

4. Double space between paragraphs in block style letter

5. Use accepted postal abbreviations for states. (VT)

III. PARAGRAPHS

PARA 1, Unity

1. <u>Mental models, our conceptual models of the ways objects work, events take place, or people behave, result from our tendency to form explanations of things</u>. These models are essential in helping us understand our experiences, predict the outcomes of our actions, and handle unexpected occurrences. ~~Unexpected occurrences can happen at any time.~~ We base our models on whatever knowledge we have, real or imaginary, naïve or sophisticated.

   [Source: modified from Norman, Donald A. *The Psychology of Everyday Things*. NY: Basic, 1988. 38.]

2. <u>The market is as much a part of your company as you are</u>. After all, it represents one-half of the ledger. To grow, your business must earn the permission of the marketplace. No concept is more important for the start-up entrepreneur. ~~Guarantees are an essential component.~~ The customer must give your business permission to sell to him. He does this (at least as a repeat customer) only after a thorough assessment of you, your product or service, and your operation. This is why Detroit is having trouble selling cars even though they're better built than they were. ~~Fortunately this hasn't been a problem in the U.S. aerospace industry.~~ These cars have to overcome years of bad notices. It will take time to accomplish this. In fact, it may take until there's a complete turnover in the market— until those of us who now think Japanese or German no longer drive.

   [Source; modified from Hawken, Paul. *Growing a Business*. NY: Simon & Schuster, 1987. 175–176.]

3. <u>A classical understanding sees the world primarily as underlying form itself. A romantic understanding sees it primarily in terms of immediate appearance.</u> If you were to show an engine or a mechanical drawing or an electronic schematic to a romantic it is unlikely he would see much in it. It has no appeal because the reality he sees is its surface. Dull, complex lists of names, lines and numbers. Nothing interesting. ~~Classification systems may say more about their creators than about the objects being classified.~~ But if you were to show the same blueprint or schematic or give the same description to a classical person, he might look at it and then become fascinated by it because he sees that within the lines and shapes and symbols is a tremendous richness of underlying form.

   [Source: modified from Pirsig, Robert M. *Zen and the Art of Motorcycle Maintenance*. NY: Bantam, 1974. 66.]

4. <u>At a certain season of our life we are accustomed to consider every spot as the possible site of a house</u>. I have thus surveyed the country on every side within a dozen miles of where I live. In imagination I have bought all the farms in succession, for all were to be bought, and I knew their price. ~~I enjoy walking and find it a healthful relaxation.~~ I walked over each farmer's premises, tasted his wild apples, discoursed on husbandry with him, and took his farm at his price.

[Source: modified from Thoreau, H.D. *Walden*. Princeton: PUP, 1971. 81.]

5. As the rules of chess define the game of chess, <u>linguistic rules define the game of language, which would not exist without them</u>. They are not strict mechanism of cause and effect—one thing simply making another thing happen—but a system essentially open and incomplete, so that it is always capable of novelty. Rules of etiquette close off a system, keeping it uniform and predictable unless the rules are changed. ~~Who is allowed to changes these rules? When can such changes be made?~~ Rules of language are indirect and can be used again and again on the same finite set of letters and words, making possible an open universe of new sentences on the closed universe of the dictionary. ~~Dictionaries you will have noticed are printed, not spoken.~~

[Source: modified from Campbell, *Jeremy. Grammatical Man*. NY: Simon & Schuster. 1982. 127.]

PARA 2b, Development Strategies 1

1. Donald Norman's *The Psychology of Everyday Things*:

    definition; cause and effect

2. Paul Hawken's *Growing a Business*:

    definition; examples

3. Robert Pirsig's *Zen and the Art of Motorcycle Maintenance*:

    classification; contrast

4. Henry David Thoreau's *Walden*:

    narration

5. Jeremy Campbell's *Grammatical Man*.

    analogy; comparison; examples

PARA 2b, Development Strategies 2

Many different strategies could be used, depending on the information you gather, your approach to the material, and your audience. Here are some possibilities:

1. definition; comparison and contrast; facts and statistics

2. definition; comparison and contrast

3. facts and statistics (to quantify recycling); cause and effect (to discuss the rate of adoption)

4. definition, likely including facts and statistics; cause and effect

5. comparison and contrast; narration

PARA 3, Coherence

See your instructor.

IV. SENTENCE CLARITY AND STYLE

CLARITY AND STYLE 1, Parallelism

Possible rewrites:

1. We will see Rufus on Tuesday and Tito on Wednesday.

2. Though he could not swim, he would not wear a life jacket.

3. El Niño has remained active in the Pacific, and the rain has continued to fall.

4. Congress has forgotten both the individual citizen and personal responsibility.

5. As the sun rose, the moon set.

CLARITY AND STYLE 2, Misplaced and Dangling Modifiers

Possible rewrites:

1. The tools Don returned to Phil were covered with grease.

2. The EPA wrote new rules for the spotted owl, which was threatened with extinction.

3. I saw him on the green walkway.

4. Young and inexperienced, Jim discovered that jobs were few and far between.

5. I wrote directions to the house for my friend.

CLARITY AND STYLE 3a, Shifts 1

See instructor for other possible answers.

1. The United Nations' membership has grown steadily, and it adds one or more new members nearly every year. (number shift)

2. When a person studies, she or he usually works for at least three hours. (person shift)

   OR When you study, you need to work for at least three hours.

3. Once people swim in this lake, especially in August, they never want to swim anywhere else. (person shift)

4. My father worked for forty-two years at General Motors. The corporation made him retire last month. (person shift)

5. When a person takes the train to St. Louis, she or he should leave by 10:37. (person shift) — or— When people take the train to St. Louis, they should leave by 10:37.

CLARITY AND STYLE 3b, Shifts 2

See instructor for other possible answers.

1. The Mississippi River carries soil that travels to other bodies of water.

2. At exactly midnight, the fireworks display started, music played, and a gunshot rang in the New Year.

3. Tomorrow we will walk to school but will ride the bus home.

4. Dogs love to play with their tails, which they chase around in circles.

5. While Melissa washed her hair, the doorbell rang.

CLARITY AND STYLE 3d, Shifts 3

See instructor for other possible answers.

1. I went to the new restaurant on Elm Street and enjoyed the meal. (subject shift)

2. The entire class read the newspaper, and then we discussed it. (voice shift)

3. As I read the newspaper, I found the story interesting. (subject shift)

4. We sat on the broken down bus until the Transit Authority sent a replacement. (subject shift: dangling modifier)

5. The family went to the beach to swim, and they had fun playing in the sand, too. (voice shift)

CLARITY AND STYLE 4a, Irrelevant Detail

1. Marx said that religion is the opium of the people.

2. Charles Dickens was a prolific author, working on up to three novels at the same time.

3. In the last six months, our newly elected president has created 2.6 million jobs.

4. Last Thanksgiving, Chuck visited his relatives.

5. The interstate highway system is now badly in need of extensive rebuilding.

CLARITY AND STYLE 4b, Mixed or Illogical Constructions

1. He said that the new bridge won't increase anybody's taxes.

2. They chatted like two birds until they tired.

3. The baker made a triple chocolate cake; however, he forgot to add baking powder.

4. My brother wrote me a letter last week, and I read it two or three times.

5. I don't know anything about Wagner's opera *Parsifal*.

CLARITY AND STYLE 5a, Subordination—Choppy Sentences

Possible rewrites:

1. Bill and Metsa, who started dating five years ago in high school, think they will get married next year.

2. Because Dwayne Wade is so fast, he plays both offense and defense well.

3. I do my research at our university library because its one million plus volumes provide coverage that is both in-depth and up-to-date.

4. Stirring constantly to ensure that the butter will not brown, heat the sauce over a low flame.

5. The Statue of Liberty, a gift from the French people and dedicated in 1886, was restored for its centennial and once again looks beautiful.

CLARITY AND STYLE 5c, Coordination—Ideas of Equal Importance

Possible rewrites:

1. I had a lot of reading to do every day; therefore, I did not watch television at all for months.

2. She agrees with many things Roberto tells her, but when she does not, she argues with him.

3. My great-uncle neither smokes nor drinks.

4. He likes not only classical music but also country and western.

5. This rain is good for people; it is filling the reservoirs.

CLARITY AND STYLE 6b, Logical Order

Possible rewrites:

1. We arrived at the Grand Canyon, loaded our packs, and hiked to the Colorado River a mile below.

2. Bonds had a terrible day when we were at the ballpark; he struck out in the first, fifth, and seventh innings.

3. I like a movie if it begins well, has a good story, and ends happily.

4. In the next three hours, I need to mow the lawn, shower and shave, and dress for a date.

5. As I looked at the Statue of Liberty, I saw the feet, the crown, and the torch.

OR As I looked at the Statue of Liberty, I saw the torch, the crown, and the feet.

CLARITY AND STYLE 6c, Active Voice

Possible rewrites:

1. Paul was bitten by mosquitoes, black flies, and chiggers on his canoe trip down the Allagash River.

2. Rodriguez hit the ball deep to center.

3. The family bought a new puppy.

4. Kurt's birthday was celebrated by everyone in our dorm.

5. Patrick called me as soon as he returned to Seattle.

CLARITY AND STYLE 7a, Sentence Variety 1

Possible rewrites:

1. Because it rained for a month, there was great flooding.

2. Vermont has a long winter, but now that I ski it seems shorter.

3. After singing in church every Sunday for years, my parents stopped last year, and now they miss it.

4. As you fly over any major U.S. city, look out the plane's window; you will be shocked by the number of swimming pools you will see.

5. Up at 5 a.m. every day, Anne never misses her gymnastics practice.

CLARITY AND STYLE 7b, Sentence Variety 2

Possible rewrites:

1. To fulfill the course requirements in Composition I, Sally wrote her research paper and handed it in to her teacher.

2. Fulfilling the course requirements in Composition I, Sally wrote her research paper and handed it in to her teacher.

3. Because she wanted to fulfill the course requirements in Composition I, Sally wrote her research paper and handed it in to her teacher.

4. In Composition I, Sally wrote her research paper and handed it in to her teacher to fulfill the course requirements.

V. WORD CHOICE

WORD 1, Eliminating Clutter

Possible answers:

1. Tom is a point guard who can play center when necessary.

2. The test was difficult because it covered the whole semester.

3. Bad weather in Atlanta delayed Bill's two brothers' flight, so we had to wait at the airport for them for five hours.

4. The school band, obviously unpracticed, could not even play the national anthem without mistakes.

5. Why do schools of swimming fish and flocks of flying birds move with a similar coordinated motion?

WORD 2c, General versus Specific Words

Possible answers:

1. transportation: bus

2. foods: vegetables

3. vegetables: carrots

4. seasons: fall

5. holidays: New Year's Day

WORD 2c, Abstract versus Concrete Words

1. pretty: abstract

2. justice: abstract

3. leaves: concrete

4. blue: abstract

5. stars: concrete

WORD 2d, Idioms

1. The committee agreed to the plan.

2. Frieda left early so that she would be sure to get a good seat.

3. My niece insisted that Jell-O was superior to pudding.

4. Though we arrived early, we still had to wait in line.

5. The coach gave me some extra tips to help me try to improve my shot.

WORD 3a-b, Appropriate Formality

Possible answers:

1. Reggie intensely disliked their new album.

2. Bryan cannot come today.

3. The show was spectacular.

4. Collecting stamps was Phil's hobby.

5. If I have time, I'll eat lunch with you at noon.

WORD 4, Bias in Writing

Possible answers:

1. Our firefighters showed great courage while battling the blaze.

2. The president was swamped with questions from the reporters.

3. The safety course was tailored to mail carriers.

4. Who chairs that Senate subcommittee?

5. Of all creatures on the planet, people are the most intelligent and the most destructive.

WORD 5, The Dictionary

1. There are four syllables in *ob•liv•i•ous*, and there are three in *ob•nox•ious*.

2. *marathon*: a race of 26 miles, 385 yards, based upon the length of the run made by a single runner from the Greek city Marathon to Athens to tell of the Greek victory (490 B.C.) over the Persians.

3. *lens* from the Latin *lentil* for the resemblance of a lens to the shape of the lentil bean. The double-convex lens.

4. *frankfurter*: a sausage originating in Frankfurt, Germany.

5. There are three syllables in *scru•pu•lous*.

WORD 6, The Thesaurus

1. **beautiful** (adj): admirable; alluring; attractive; appealing; splendid

   (antonym): ugly

2. **show** (noun); drama; performance; demonstration; exposition; fair (verb): bare; reveal; exhibit; expose; divulge

   (antonym): (verb) hide

3. **nice** (adjective): fine, pleasant, satisfactory, good-natured, amiable, friendly

   (antonym): awkward, bad, insensitive, awful

4. **document** (noun): certificate; charter; deed; form; instrument

   (verb): chronicle; list; log; note; write down

   (antonym): (verb) destroy records

5. **industrious** (adj): busy; conscientious; assiduous; diligent; earnest

   (antonym): lazy

VI. PARTS & PATTERNS

PARTS & PATTERNS 1a, Verbs

1. Tina <u>swims</u> in the pool on Tuesdays.

VI

2. John <u>gave</u> <u>Fred</u> <u>a birthday present.</u>

        VT IO   DO

3. The weather <u>seems</u> <u>fine</u> today.

             VI PA

4. Shelby <u>bought</u> <u>her textbooks</u> at the campus bookstore.

         VT   DO

5. Jorge <u>is</u> <u>a tenor.</u>

       VI PN

PARTS & PATTERNS 1a, Nouns

	singular	**plural**	**sing. possessive**	**pl. possessive**
1.	dish	dishes	dish's	dishes'
2.	hero	heroes	hero's	heroes'
3.	book	books	book's	books'
4.	wife	wives	wife's	wives'
5.	man	men	man's	men's

PARTS & PATTERNS 1a, Pronouns

1. <u>I</u> gave Donald a call.

2. <u>I</u> spoke to <u>him</u> yesterday.

3. <u>He</u> usually has to call <u>me</u> back.

4. Raspberries are ready at <u>their</u> farm.

5. <u>Which</u> farm do <u>you</u> visit?

PARTS & PATTERNS 1a, Adjectives

1. If presented with Häagen-Dazs and Ben & Jerry's ice creams, could you say which is (creamy, <u>creamier</u>, creamiest)?

2. The *Washington Post* declined to name the (good, better, <u>best</u>) candidate among the five potential nominees.

3. Jack is (old, <u>older</u>, oldest) than his brother John.

4. Jack is the (old, older, <u>oldest</u>) of the four children.

5. Before starting the race, the judge called, "May the (good, better, <u>best</u>) cyclist win!"

PARTS & PATTERNS 1a, Adverbs

1. John runs <u>fast</u>.

2. Of all the sopranos, Lena sang the <u>most beautifully</u>.

3. The commute home <u>always</u> seemed longer than the one to the office.

4. After the thunderstorm, steam rose <u>eerily</u> from the still-warm pavement.

5. Jackson was tired but worked <u>hard</u> to finish the assigned reading before going to bed.

PARTS & PATTERNS 1a, Prepositions

1. (<u>On</u> the move) (<u>since</u> dawn), the hikers had advanced twenty miles (<u>by</u> lunchtime).

2. Sara finished three (<u>of</u> the four essay questions) quickly.

3. Chu's nieces and nephews danced (<u>around</u> the room).

4. Bill saw his quarter roll (<u>into</u> the street) and disappear (<u>down</u> a storm drain).

5. Forty-seven stories (<u>above</u> the street), the birds built their nest (<u>on</u> one) (<u>of</u> the Chrysler Building's ledges).

PARTS & PATTERNS 1a, Conjunctions

1. I went to the store (<u>before</u> Sushmito arrived). (SUB)

2. It rained all night, (<u>so</u> the tournament was postponed). (COORD)

3. I like to fish (even <u>though</u> I don't catch anything most days). (SUB)

4. (<u>Although</u> Melville's *Moby Dick* is a great book), there are some chapters that are slow reading. (SUB)

5. Professor Pham asked us (<u>not only</u> to compare and contrast Melville and Thoreau, <u>but also</u> to use one or more of their works to support our points). (CORREL)

PARTS & PATTERNS 1b, Subjects

1. Because my bearded collie, Kado, sleeps so much, <u>my roommate</u> thinks my dog is a stuffed animal.

2. <u>Ly's enthusiasm for our annual reunion</u> is infectious.

3. <u>Joan's track and swimming talents</u> earned her a scholarship.

4. <u>Calculus 201 and Chemistry 137</u> have kept me extremely busy this semester.

5. The last time I checked, <u>the university</u> had five libraries.

PARTS & PATTERNS 1b, Predicates

1. Smoking <u>is expensive and addictive.</u>

2. Juan <u>believed that his studies were a worthwhile investment</u>.

3. Melissa's research paper <u>explored the differences between personal debt and the national debt</u>.

4. Gwen <u>is the oldest of five children</u>.

5. After working together all day, Bill and Ted <u>cooked dinner together also</u>.

PARTS & PATTERNS 1b, Objects

1. Jerry washed <u>his dog</u> after it fought with a skunk. (DO)

2. My grandson brought <u>me flowers</u> for Mother's Day. (IO, DO)

3. Iris informed <u>her students</u> about the upcoming exam. (DO)

4. The student asked <u>for a better grade on her paper</u>. (DO)

5. Julia asked <u>me</u> to take her to the mall. (DO)

PARTS & PATTERNS 1c, Prepositional Phrases

1. The rabbit went (into its cage).

2. Manuel was scared (about entering his new school).

3. The stain (on her shirt) embarrassed Abigail.

4. The car (with the dent) (on the front fender) is my sister's.

5. Running laps (around the block) became boring (for the track star).

PARTS & PATTERNS 1c, Verbals

1. I love <u>running</u> because it requires so little equipment. (GER)

2. <u>Pacing yourself</u> during an exam is crucial. (GER)

3. The drummer <u>playing the steel drums</u> is my cousin. (PRES PART)

4. The Continental Army, <u>faced with many hardships</u>, managed <u>to defeat</u> <u>the better trained and equipped British</u>. (PAST PART; INF; PAST PART)

5. <u>To conduct good science</u> requires first, good <u>training</u>: second, good insight; and third, great effort. (INF; GER)

PARTS & PATTERNS 1d, Clauses

1. <u>When I saw Roger</u>, <u>who was just returning from a trip</u>, he told me <u>he would be playing softball with us this Saturday</u>. (ADV CLS: ADJ CLS: NOUN CLS)

2. Ceilia painted her house purple <u>because it was her favorite color</u>. (ADV CLS)

3. <u>If you hit or tip a ball foul and you already have two strikes</u>, the count remains unchanged. (ADV CLS)

4. He hoped <u>his contribution to the charity would benefit [whoever was most in need]</u>. (NOUN CLS [NOUN CLS])

5. After losing three games straight, the team was ecstatic <u>when it beat the undefeated first place team</u>. (ADV CLS)

PARTS & PATTERNS 1e, Types of Sentences

1. Though ordinary ink may look black, it also contains red pigment. (complex)

2. Fred likes to read in bed. (simple)

3. *The Grapes of Wrath* and *Of Mice and Men* are examples of books read more often in high school than college. (simple)

4. After scooping ice cream all summer, my right arm was so strong that I could beat my older brother in arm wrestling, and my left arm looked so withered to me that it seemed almost like the forelegs of <u>Tyrannosaurus rex</u>. (compound-complex)

5. Though it may sound odd, l swim in the winter and ski in the summer. (complex)

PARTS & PATTERNS 2, Subject-Verb Agreement 1

1. The ticket, including dinner with dessert, a floor show, and dancing after, costs only twenty dollars.

2. The smell of the ripening apples and pears attracts bees to the orchard.

3. Neither my parents nor my brother wants to try my latest culinary triumph: cranberry-tofu meat loaf.

4. The democratic minority make their voices heard.

5. High tides and wind create dangerous conditions along the coast.

PARTS & PATTERNS 2 e-l, Subject-Verb Agreement 2

1. Anyone who studies regularly will do better in school and enjoy it more.

2. All the explanations are inadequate.

3. None of my classes meets before 10 a.m.

4. There are, on a regulation baseball team, nine players.

5. Politics both fascinates and repulses him.

PARTS & PATTERNS 3a–b, Principal Parts of Irregular Verbs

1. If you bend the pipe more, I think it will fit.

2. After John sat down, he pulled out a book and dozed off.

3. Having taken the subway for years, I was not easily surprised by unusual looking passengers.

4. Paul took the dinner roast out at noon because it was frozen.

5. I saw that new movie with Jennifer Lopez last week.

PARTS & PATTERNS 3c, Verb Tense

1. PRESENT PERFECT: I have gone to the All-Star Game every year.

2. PRESENT PROGRESSIVE: I am going to the All-Star Game this year.

3. PRESENT PERFECT PROGRESSIVE: I have been going to the All-Star Game every year.

4. PAST: I went to the All-Star Game every year until last year.

5. PAST PERFECT: I had gone to the All-Star Game every year until last year.

PARTS & PATTERNS 3e, Verb Mood

1. (indicative) Bob asked <u>that Joe come home early today</u>.

2. (subjunctive) If I were training harder, <u>I would be better prepared</u>.

3. (indicative) <u>Every night he reads until bedtime.</u>

4. (imperative) Mary said, "<u>Hurry up, or we'll miss the bus.</u>"

5. (subjunctive) <u>I wished it were snowing,</u> but it was only raining.

PARTS & PATTERNS 3f, Active and Passive Voices

1. (passive) The letters were mailed by Jamal after lunch.

2. (active) Raoul cooked the dinner.

3. (passive) *Angle of Repose* was written by Wallace Stegner.

4. (passive) The Blue Line bus was seen by Regina.

5. (active) Many people who rarely watch baseball otherwise watch the World Series.

PARTS & PATTERNS 4a, Pronoun Agreement

1. The jury provided its decision to the judge.

2. He needs to better train his dog Biff, who barks at the letter carrier every day.

3. Neither of the girls can baby-sit her little sister.

4. When Louisa and Hal come to visit, they always bring their dog.

5. Each player in the tournament took a turn at the table.

PARTS & PATTERNS 4b, Pronoun Reference

1. I'm concerned about your grades. (Note: you may insert other ideas for the word *that*.)

2. Professor Tecknor, who studies psychology and relationships, gave a lecture on them at our seminar.

3. Though I know that supply-side economics focuses on production, and demand-side economics emphasizes consumption, this knowledge has never helped me understand where my paycheck goes every week.

4. When the company demanded a cut in wages and benefits, the union leadership recommended a strike vote be taken.

5. When tours come through our town, they often stop at the Shelburne Museum to see its extensive American folk art collection.

PARTS & PATTERNS 4c, Pronoun Case 1

1. Have you seen my brother?

2. After taking the train, Chuck and I went to the deli.

3. If it were up to Laura and me, we'd leave now.

4. The boss appreciated their working on Saturday night.

5. My sister said she would be going to visit our grandmother after visiting Susan and me.

PARTS & PATTERNS 4c–d, Pronoun Case 2

1. Professor Malcolm asked Dave and me to participate in the experiment.

2. Despite all his campaigning, the incumbent was running stronger than he, as the *New York Times* reported.

3. My sister, who has incredibly acute hearing when it comes to the telephone, yelled out from the shower, "Whom is that call for?"

4. Our best hitter came to the plate with two runners on, Lana and me.

5. The victory will go to whomever wins.

PARTS & PATTERNS 5, Adjectives and Adverbs

1. Laura grew more and more confident as the semester progressed.

2. I think it's colder today than yesterday.

3. The CIA is charged with monitoring these kinds of sensitive security issues.

4. He is doing well in pottery class.

5. With two of their starters on the disabled list, things look bad for the Seattle Mariners.

PARTS & PATTERNS 6, Sentence Fragments 1

Possible rewrites:

1. S, F: Rhonda ran to the store because she needed milk.

2. F: The big, black dog was prancing down the crowded sidewalk.

3. F: As long as you support your point, you can write a good argument.

4. S

5. F, S: The cat that climbed the tree is a stray.

PARTS & PATTERNS 6, Sentence Fragments 2

Possible rewrites:

1. My little brother is 6' 2" and still growing.

2. My big brother Todd likes to dance, especially to hip-hop music.

3. While on vacation, I read two books: Nicholas Evans's *The Horse Whisperer* and Frances Mayes's *Under the Tuscan Sun*.

4. Last night I saw Neville and Molly at the student union.

5. When I saw the *Mona Lisa* in person, I was, to be honest, disappointed.

PARTS AND PATTERNS 7, Comma Splices 1

Possible rewrites:

1. Margaret is getting married on Saturday. I hope it doesn't rain then.

2. Professor Gerson has a pleasantly acid sense of humor; accordingly, he quipped that the term *European ally* is an oxymoron.

3. I practice piano one hour every day; this has helped me improve a lot in the last year.

4. Spring in San Francisco is cool, and many visitors wish they had brought warmer clothes.

5. I am a business major, so studying economics will give me a useful background.

PARTS & PATTERNS 7, Comma Splices 2

Possible rewrites:

1. The days are beginning to get longer, and there's more sun every day.

2. With all the channel choices on cable and satellite TV these days, I wish there were something good to watch. It seems like there were better programs when I had fewer choices.

3. Can you read this? I don't have my glasses with me.

4. They weren't important ideas; however, they were interesting suggestions.

5. I didn't know what I wanted to study in college because I had too many choices, and I felt confused.

PARTS AND PATTERNS 7, Run-on Sentences 1

Possible rewrites:

1. We took a cab to the theatre. We saw *Rent*.

2. I hope Ben will come over and help me adjust my car's carburetor.

3. After it rained for twenty days straight, I felt like escaping to the desert.

4. I know what an armadillo looks like, but I'm not quite sure what an aardvaark looks like.

5. The last U.S. space shuttle flight to *Mir* was made in 1999; since then, all shuttle flights have been to the new International Space Station.

PARTS AND PATTERNS 7, Run-on Sentences 2

Possible rewrites:

1. The audience cheered as the actors bowed.

2. The guitarist was excellent, and the girl sang well, too.

3. Janel got an A on her essay, so she must have written many drafts.

4. By then, the baby was asleep, but the mother was too tired to cook.

5. In the waiting room, a man was reading a book while a woman was watching TV.

VII. PUNCTUATION

PUNCT 1a–c, The Comma 1

1. He worked hard, yet he was not feeling tired.

2. As Felix watched, the cat ate her breakfast of Tuna Delight.

3. Last semester, I had Professor Roop for history, which has always been my favorite subject.

4. Yawning, Marlena put down her book and went to bed.

5. My oldest brother, Geoffrey, usually comes for Thanksgiving.

PUNCT 1d–g, The Comma 2

1. The recipe specifically called for three large red tomatoes.

2. This fall Eliot was reading Ernest Hemingway, Maya Angelou, and Alice Walker.

3. For this reason, the committee voted to change the policy.

4. President Jimmy Carter may turn out to be more effective out of office than in, unlike Lyndon Johnson.

5. Riding into a headwind can help you improve your cycling endurance, power, and technique.

PUNCT 1h–l, The Comma 3

1. I smiled and said, "Yes, I'll be there."

2. If you want to call, Jessica has a phone.

3. Our reservations are for Friday, October 26, through Sunday, November 11.

4. Luke called yesterday and said, "Congratulations on your new baby."

5. Lonnie gave me a ride from Tulsa, Oklahoma, to Paris, Texas.

PUNCT 1m, The Comma 4

1. Adela and her brother watched *Lost* every week.

2. I drove last week to Pullman, Washington, to visit my best friends.

3. Reviewers are critical of comedies like *Two and a Half Men*.

4. If I were you, I would leave before rush hour.

5. The small gold locket was a family heirloom.

PUNCT 2, The Semicolon

1. The drive from Akron to Cincinnati was long, but I didn't mind, nor did my sister.

2. The rapid decrease in computer hardware prices has put pressure on software developers to do the same; nonetheless, they have resisted the trend for the most part.

3. On one recent weekend I saw *Pearl Harbor*, which used extensive computer-generated simulations of an historical event; *The Matrix*, which explored virtual worlds accessed via mind control; and *Until the End of the World*, which presented computer-driven dream exploration.

4. I was shocked when I drove the $20,000 car; it rode only a bit better than my current car, which has a book value of only $1,500.

5. Although I support universal access to health care, I disagree with combining it with a flat rate; providing access shouldn't eliminate government support entirely.

PUNCT 3, The Colon

1. I have passed along to my children one of my father's sayings: "When you borrow something, try to return it in better condition than you received it."

2. Scientists, in an effort to isolate what it is in food that makes most people evaluate it as "tasting good or delicious," have determined the single most important ingredient: fat.

3. On your way home, please pick up a pound of cold cuts, a head of lettuce, and a video.

4. Today is a very good day for haying: plenty of sunshine, a light breeze, and low humidity.

5. We took the following route: Route 80 to Rock Springs, Route 187 to Farson, and Route 28 to South Pass City.

PUNCT 4, The Apostrophe

1. Did you see the film *My Mother's Castle*?

2. My grandmother told me that the '38 hurricane was much worse than this year's storm.

3. A snake sheds its skin when it's growing.

4. What is our company's policy regarding maternity leave?

5. I thought it was hers, but perhaps it's really Bill's.

PUNCT 5, Quotation Marks

1. "Where you place your commas is one of my teacher's pet peeves, so I always double check my work," said Elaine.

2. "Would you like to come to dinner with us?" Mary asked.

3. When I read computer magazines, I find all the technobabble confusing: RAM, ROM, and bytes. Who dreams up these terms?

4. Milan told me that Faulkner wrote the novel *As I Lay Dying* in only six weeks.

5. "I hope you'll come to our party tonight," said Alison.

   "Me too," I replied, "but I have to work until 11."

   "That's no problem," she said. "It doesn't even start until 10, and I doubt you'll miss anything. Just come as you are after work."

PUNCT 6a, The Period

1. If you know the Latin meaning abbreviated by a.m. and p.m., you will find it easier to remember which one to use.

2. One of the experimental drugs being used to combat AIDS is AZT.

3. I wondered if he knew what the USDA stamp on the meat stood for.

4. One of the most woeful scenes in all of Shakespeare is in *King Lear*.

5. Tintin's best friend is Capt. Horatio Haddock.

PUNCT 6b–c, The Question Mark and Exclamation Point

1. Joyce said, "Do you know whether bus or subway is the better way to get to Avenue J from here?"

2. As usual for this region, the weather was sunny.

3. Which route to Des Moines has less traffic, John wanted to know.

4. "Can I come too?" my sister asked.

5. Louis asked me which class I liked best.

PUNCT 6d–h, Other Punctuation

Possible Rewrites:

1. One awkward, but acceptable, solution to the problem of sexism in pronouns is the use of *him/her* as well as *he or she*.

2. When in Rome—as the saying goes—do as the Romans do.

3. In her research paper, Elizabeth quoted Sam Jones, "The incidence of Alzheimer's increases with ages [sic] and more with women than men."

4. "Our class meets in that new science building. What's its name? Something Hall ... Burstein ... Gurstein? I can't remember," said John.

5. I still remember the opening lines of Shakespeare's Sonnet LXXIII: "That time of year thou mayst in me behold / When yellow leaves, or none, or few, do hang / Upon those boughs which shake against the cold."

VIII. MECHANICS

MECH 1a–d, Capitals 1

1. Unfortunately, stargazers living this far south can't see the North Star.

2. When James "Joe" Jackson sang last week at the Hartford Avenue Grill, the crowd roared its approval.

3. The cold war may be over, but we're still paying the bill.

4. The Baptist church in my town sponsors a community food bank.

5. In the last four months, the Missouri and Mississippi rivers reached record flood levels, but the Hudson River was below normal.

MECH 1e–j, Capitals 2

1. In a recent article, commentator Julia Webb wrote, "For the first time in U.S. history, by the year 2002, more than fifty percent of all American jobs will require at least one year of college."

2. I read the *Daily Plains Record* every day to keep up on local news.

3. During the spring semester, Dennis is going to enroll in calculus, history, and English.

4. I think she bought one of the new Apple notebook computers.

5. Who reports on the news media? The news media do.

MECH 2, Abbreviations

1. He reported to Sergeant Bilko.

2. The president announced that the new policy was designed to protect our national security.

3. Aristotle was born in 384 B C.

4. Dr. C. Everett Koop gave the keynote address.—or—

   C. Everett Koop, M.D., gave the keynote address. [MD and M.D. are both acceptable]

5. For the trip, they packed clothes, food, games, and so forth.
   —OR— For the trip, they packed clothes, food, games, etc.

MECH 3, Numbers

1. Armand cut the plank into 4 six-foot sections. [or four 6-foot sections]

2. Charles Lindbergh began his historic two-day flight on May 20, 1927, from Roosevelt Field, Long Island.

3. Scott thought the boat out to Catalina Island cost more than $20 [or twenty dollars].

4. American Airlines currently has over 620 planes.

5. Over the holidays we saw four films, two plays, and thirteen videos. [or 4 films, 2 plays, and 13 videos]

MECH 4, Italics/Underlining

1. Linda likes Microsoft <u>Word</u>, but I prefer <u>WordPerfect.</u>

2. The most commonly occurring word in English is <u>the</u>. .

3. I asked him to explain what <u>noblesse oblige</u> means.

4. Did you read last week's cover story in <u>Newsweek</u>?

5. Tina objected to Dickens's frequent use of a <u>deus ex machina</u> to resolve his fantastically-plotted novels. .

MECH 5, The Hyphen

1. I am very close to my brother-in-law.

2. The ex-Metropolitan Opera soprano joined our community chorus and improved the entire section's performance.

3. Are you looking forward to the beginning of the school year?

4. Our class voted twenty-one to seventeen for more study time.

5. In pre-revolutionary America, the colonists were subjects of the king of England.

MECH 6a, Basic Spelling Rules

1. I'm hoping we can see Jeri before she leaves.

2. Professor Guimard is very knowledgeable about plate tectonics.

3. Lorraine was lying down thinking when an idea suddenly occurred to her; half an hour later she had laid out all the fundamentals in the field of astronomy.

4. How much did you say you paid for those peaches?

5. I sent the package via Federal Express, so he ought to receive it by noon tomorrow.

MECH 6b, Words that Sound Alike

1. When I reached the library, I was gasping for breath.

2. In the 100-meter finals, Sarah was third and I was fourth.

3. My father is site manager for the new Deeter Building construction project.

4. My teacher recommended that we always read the foreword, as it usually defines the scope and approach of the book that follows.

5. All the people I know with personal stationery are of my parents' generation.

IX. RESEARCH WRITING

Research exercises are incorporated into chapter XI, MLA-Style Documentation, and Format; chapter XII, APA-Style Documentation, and Format; and chapter XIII, CMS Documentation and Format/CSE Documentation.

X. WRITING IN THE DISCIPLINES

WRIT DISCIPLINES 1a Understand Your Writing Assignment

Answers will vary by student. See your instructor for assistance.

WRIT DISCIPLINES 1b, 1e Methods/Evidence and Documentation/Format

1. Primary sources are original documents written or captured by those who experienced and witnessed events firsthand. Examples will vary by student.

2. Secondary sources are documents one or more steps removed from the events or objects which are their subjects. Examples will vary by student.

WRIT DISCIPLINES 2d Conventions for Writing about Literature

See your instructor.

WRIT DISCIPLINES 2d, 3d, 4d, and 5d Conventions

All Disciplines

    1. first, second

Literature

   2.   summarizing

Humanities

   5.   principles of historic

Social Sciences

   7.   valid, reliable, and random

Natural and Applied Sciences

   9.   objective or scientific, and passive rather than active

XI. MLA-STYLE DOCUMENTATION AND FORMAT

MLA-Style Documentation and Format Questions

1.   Modern Language Association

2.   in-text citations and works cited page

3.   They immediately let readers know the source of a citation without breaking the flow of the paper.

4.   author's last name and page number

5.   Two or three authors must include all authors' names within the signal phrase or in the parentheses; for works with more than three authors, include only the last name of the first author, followed by the Latin phrase *et al.*

MLA, Avoiding Plagiarism

Because there are infinitely many possible correct paraphrases of the quotations provided, it is left to the instructor to review and assess each student's work for this exercise.

MLA, Integrating Borrowed Material.

Because there are infinitely many possible correct ways to incorporate these quotations, it is left to the instructor to review and assess each student's work for this exercise.

MLA 1a, In-Text Citations

Note: Possible answers are provided, but many other valid solutions exist.

1. The fantasy genre has always supported the concept of a separate, sometimes superior, animal wisdom: "Human beings say, 'It never rains but it pours.' This is not very apt, for it frequently does rain without pouring. The rabbits' proverb is better expressed. They say, 'One cloud feels lonely'" (Adams 184).

2. The fantasy genre has always supported the concept of a separate, sometimes superior, animal wisdom. In *Watership Down*, Richard Adams's narrator gently chides the reader: "Human beings say, 'It never rains but it pours.' This is not very apt, for it frequently does rain without pouring. The rabbits' proverb is better expressed. They say, 'One cloud feels lonely'" (184).

3. Though they exist in infinite variety, clouds have a simple shared origin: "A cloud is a collection of water droplets or ice crystals in the air. It is formed when water vapor is cooled and changed into water droplets or ice crystals" (Heimler and Neal 234).

4. Heimler and Neal point out in *Principles* that though clouds exist in infinite variety, they have a simple shared origin: "A cloud is a collection of water droplets or ice crystals in the air. It is formed when water vapor is cooled and changed into water droplets or ice crystals" (234).

5. As Symington observed, "NATO's muddled expansion is so fraught with competing strategies that it has simultaneously threatened Moscow and made overtures to Russia to join the alliance itself" ("Crossroads" 267).

MLA 2, Manuscript Format

   (a) <u>top of page</u> to <u>last name/page number</u>: 1/2 inch

1. (b) top and bottom margins: 1 inch

2 (c) line spacing: double-spaced

3. (d) left margin: 1 inch

4. (e) right margin: 1 inch

5. (f) "Smith page 3" should instead be "Smith 3"— "page" shouldn't be written out.

MLA 1c, Formatting a Works Cited Page

Works Cited

Hamlet. 26 Feb. 2007 http://www.shakespeare-literature.com/Hamlet/index.html.

Massie, Allan. "Prince of Self-Pity." *Spectator* 65.1 (2006): 4+. Expanded Academic Index. InfoTrac. 26 Feb. 2007.

McManaway, James Gilmere. Shakespeare 400: Essays by American Scholars on the Anniversary of the Poet's Birth. NY: Holt, Rinehart, and Winston, 1964.

XII. APA-STYLE DOCUMENTATION AND FORMAT

APA, Style Documentation and Format Questions

1. American Psychological Association

2. brief in-text citation and reference page

3. They immediately let readers know the source of a citation without breaking the flow of the paper.

4. author's last name, year of publication

5. For two authors, list both authors' names in the text with year of publication immediately following, or put both names in a parenthetical citation, using an ampersand between the names. For three to five authors, give all authors' last names in the text or parentheses in your first citation only. Use an ampersand instead of *and* in the parenthetical citation. In subsequent citations, use only the first author's name and *et al.* For a work with six or more authors, in all citations, use the first author's name, followed by *et al.*

APA 2, Manuscript Format

(a) top of page to Title/page number: 1/2 inch

1. (b) top and bottom margins: 1 inch

2. (c) line spacing: double-spaced

3. (d) left margin: 1 inch

4. (e) right margin: 1 inch

5. (f) "Smith page 3" should instead be "Rise and Fall 3"--the student's name is not included, nor is the word "page," and the page number should be preceded by a shortened version of the paper's title (here given as "Rise and Fall").

APA Reference Page

References

Brandt, D. (2001). *Literacy in American lives.* New York: Cambridge University Press.

Glazebrook, T. (2000). From…to nature, artifacts to technology: Heidegger on Aristotle, Galileo, and Newton. *The Southern Journal of Philosophy,*

Greengard, S. (1999). Getting rid of the paper chase. *Workforce*, p. 69. Retrieved February 24, 2002, from InfoTrac (General Business File ASAP database).

XIII. CMS Documentation and Format/CSE Documentation

CMS Questions

1. *The Chicago Manual of Style*

2. series of raised Arabic numerals placed after each item being acknowledged that refer to endnotes at the end of the paper; and a bibliography that provides complete data for sources cited in the paper as well as some consulted but not actually cited

3. They let readers know that a source is used.

4. Elements include complete publication data, including the page number for the material you are quoting, paraphrasing, or summarizing.

5. Use normal order for all names after the first, using commas to separate the names with an *and* before the last author's name

CMS Bibliography

Bibliography

Anbinder, Tyler. "Which Poor Man's Fight? Immigrants and the Federal Conscription of 1863." Civil War History, December 2006, http://80-find.galegroup.com/ (accessed March 15, 2007).

Hlatky, Mark A. et al. "Quality-of-Life and Depressive Symptoms." Journal of the American Medical Association, 6 February 2002. http://jama.ama-assn.org (accessed January 7, 2007).

Niederkorn, William S. "A Scholar Recants on His 'Shakespeare Discovery.'" New York Times, June 20, 2002, Arts section, Midwest edition.

CSE Questions

1. Council of Science Editors

2. a brief in-text reference at the point of each borrowing and a list of references at the end of the paper that provide complete bibliographical information for the sources cited in the text

3. CSE citation-sequence system, CSE name-year system, CSE citation-name system

4. Provide the last name of the authors and the year of publication in parentheses. If there are two authors, use *and* between the names. For three or more authors, use the first author's last name followed by *et al.*

5. References or Cited References

CSE References Page

Cited References

1. Philippi TE, Dixon PM, Taylor BE. Detecting trends in species composition. Eco Appl [serial on the Internet]. 1998 May [cited 2007 Mar 15]; 8: 300-8. Available from: http://www.esajournals.org/esaonline

2. Hilton-Taylor C. 2000 IUCN red list of threatened species [serial on the Internet]. 2000 [cited 2007 Apr 2]; available from: http://www.redlist.org

3. Mech LD. The arctic wolf: living with the pack. Stillwater (MN): Voyageur Press; 1998. 128 p.

XIV. ESL BASICS

AN IMPORTANT REMINDER FOR STUDENTS: Because of the flexibility of the English language, there may be more than one way to correct the errors in each exercise. This is particularly true in this chapter. If you have any questions about your answers versus the ones supplied in the Selected Answers section, please ask your instructor. Very likely there will be other students with the same or similar questions.

ESL 1a, Modals

1. In one hour I will be done.

2. You will see me there tonight.

3. I should be able to finish this novel before class. —or—

   I can finish this novel before class.

4. We cannot come to the party.

5. When I was growing up, my family usually would take a trip in the summer.

ESL 1b, Perfect Tenses

1. They have traveled too much this year to want to go on another trip soon.

2. We had expected you yesterday.

3. Bill goes to the movies frequently; he will have seen that one already.

4. Chloë had sung in the choir for three years before she was chosen to be its director.

5. Suzanne has brought me flowers every year on my birthday.

ESL 1c, Progressive Tenses

1. John is seeing Reno for the first time.

2. Sheila is giving her friends dancing lessons.

3. The ozone layer has been thinning because of the release of harmful chemicals.

4. Han is happy today.

5. Sanga had been thinking calculus was easy until he took the midterm exam.

ESL 1d, Passive Voice 1

1. The NBA championship was won by San Antonio this year.

2. Africa is visited by many Americans.

3. We were seated by the hostess.

4. Many books now are published only in paperback.

5. Every student is expected to do well in his or her studies.

ESL 1d, Passive Voice 2

1. Terusuke lost my backpack yesterday.

2. Every day many commuters see the fountain.

3. Bizet wrote *Carmen*.

4. Many people enjoy reading.

5. My parents saved money scrupulously.

ESL 1e, Two-Word Verbs

1. Where's the newspaper? Oh, John threw it away.

2. The teacher called on the student.

3. Because of the extensive fire damage, the fire marshal ordered the building's owners to tear it down.

4. Simone heard from her best friend.

5. Why doesn't he pick on someone his own size?

ESL 1f, Verbals

1. They agreed to come over here before the game.

2. Josef misses eating home-cooked meals.

3. The boss permitted me to take time off when my sister was married.

4. I imagine flying is wonderful.

5. When I finish eating, I'll read to you.

ESL 2a–c, Count and Noncount Nouns 1

1. Gordon knows a lot of local history.

2. How many loaves of bread did Orlo ask us to pick up? —or—

   How many types of bread did Orlo ask us to pick up?

3. Howard used two hundred pails of sand to build his huge sand castle.

4. Guadalupe said many machines are built there.

5. Don't put too much salt in the soup!

ESL 2a–b, Count and Noncount Nouns 2

1. Gianni lost his cash through a hole in his pocket.

2. Their new furniture is beautiful.

3. Are there many students in your history class?

4. Is Karen still looking for a place to live?

5. The poet read her poems with a lot of confidence.

ESL 2c–d, Articles

1. An hour ago he left for the office.

2. The president is the former governor of Texas.

3. When she finishes high school, she wants to travel before finding employment.

4. It was a hot day, so we went to the beach.

5. She worked for General Electric before joining Intel.

ESL 2d, Definite Article

1. Please pass the ketchup.

2. Mount Katahdin is the highest peak in Maine.

3. I saw the professor who won the Nobel Prize last year.

4. Hockey is very popular here.

5. I saw Bob walking down the hall just a minute ago.

ESL 3a, Cumulative Adjectives

1. a long white pearl necklace

2. my first new bicycle

3. five small square buildings

4. an ancient brick fireplace

5. seven large triangular windows

ESL 3b, Present and Past Participles

1. Lola found the novel's ending surprising.

2. The winter winds here are very drying.

3. Sofia found organic chemistry fascinating.

4. Jackie's remarks annoyed me.

5. The kitchen scene in *Jurassic Park* was frightening.

ESL 3c, Adverbs

1. The president traditionally addresses the Congress in January.

2. There never seems to be enough time.

3. My older sister is always helpful.

4. I drove fast enough to get to work on time.

5. Ving typically went to the museum with his father.

ESL 4a–c, Prepositions 1

1. I went to the movies nearly every week last summer.

2. Francesca reads the newspaper to improve her English.

3. When we first moved to Toronto, I missed Hong Kong very much.

4. Sari shops in the grocery store every day.

5. After his trip to Somalia, the landscape in New England looked very green to him.

ESL 4d–f, Prepositions 2

1. Frederico was aware of the problem.

2. My brother's new glasses are for reading.

3. I walked as far as Main Street before discovering that I had left my wallet at home.

4. How much is that equal to in dollars?

5. I like to paint as well as to draw.

ESL 5a–b, Omitted Verbs and Subjects

1. My school has three libraries. It will begin construction of a fourth soon. —or—

   My school has three libraries and will begin construction of a fourth soon.

2. Dirk's whole family is very amusing.

3. The baseball league begins its season next week.

4. This reading assignment is very long.

5. The crickets in the trees in my neighborhood sing all day.

ESL 5c, Expletives

1. There are three interstate highways into downtown Atlanta.

2. Here are my top choices for the position.

3. Here is the best recipe I have for turkey stuffing.

4. It is unlikely to rain when the sky is so clear.

5. There are many golf courses in Chittenden County.

ESL 6b, Questions with *Who*, *Whom*, and *What*

1. Who is coming to dinner?

2. Who created the congressional gridlock?

3. Whom did the president nominate?

4. Who brings in today's mail?

5. What does the committee do?

ESL 6c, Indirect Questions 1

1. How will they finance the new day care center?

2. Which astronomer identified black holes?

3. Why did my family come to this country in 1848?

4. Where was the smoke coming from?

5. How does the U.S. Congress differ from the British Parliament?

ESL 6c, Indirect Questions 2

1. He asked if I was coming or not.

2. Rupert wasn't sure when the Battle of Hastings occurred.

3. We tried to see where the rocket went.

4. The committee researched why the cost of education has outpaced inflation in the last ten years.

5. Everice asked whether I enjoy playing racquetball.

ESL 6d, Reported Speech

1. Nino said that he loves zucchini almost as much as he loves peppers.

2. Bob told me, "I am working in the library five nights per week."

3. With a grin, Erin stated that Roger had played a faltering but passionate cello for years.

4. Mary announced, "I will be running in the New York Marathon this year."

5. The company spokesperson said to wait for the third quarter results.

ESL 6e, Conditional Sentences

1. If he sees a shooting star, he makes a wish.

2. If you practice enough, you can join a band.

3. If I had practiced more, I might have had my own band.

4. Wherever Fleetwood Mac performed last year, they found big audiences.

5. If Al Gore had been elected, what changes would he have made?

XV GLOSSARY

GLOSSARY, Usage 1

1. I thought we could leave, but Joe is not ready to go.

2. The reason Nicholas loved music of all types is he studied music appreciation in college.

3. Although I set out twenty tomato plants this summer, I should have planted thirty.

4. Since the show on Channel 42 at 10 tonight is very interesting, he will be sure to set his TIVO to record it.

5. Jason can hardly get his work done because of school.

GLOSSARY, Usage 2

1. What are the effects of the new spending bill?

   affect: (verb) to change

   effect: (noun) a result; also (verb) to produce

2. Even if you disagree strongly with him, please be civil.

   civic: (adj) relating to a city

   civil: (adj) refraining from rudeness

3. Emile can hardly read without going to sleep.

   can't hardly: a double negative and this usage should be avoided

4. Regardless of her efforts, Jane still didn't get a raise.

   irregardless: non-standard for regardless

5. Paul, carried away by the emotional appeal of his own argument, went off on a tangent.

   tangible: (adj) something that can be touched

   tangent (go off on a tangent): (verb) to break from a line of thinking; to digress